My Garden Doctor

Originally by Frances Duncan

Patricia Lanza

Patricia Lanza
2011

Award Winning Author of *Lasagna Gardening;*
No Digging, No Tilling, No Weeding, No Kidding!

the Peppertree Press
Sarasota, Florida

Foreword

I have always loved books. As an only child for the first eight years of my life I thought of them as companions; even close friends.

In the small Tennessee town where I was born we had a library full of well-read books and most everyone had a radio. I didn't know anyone who had television.

When my brother Tommy was born I had someone to read to and when my brother Randy was born I had an audience of two.

My immediate family moved to Jacksonville, Florida when I was in my teens. We still had no TV but I quickly found the library.

I married while there in Jacksonville and had seven children. Later our family moved to Albany, Georgia. We lived in an old plantation house surrounded by three hundred acres of pecan groves. We finally had TV but nothing on the small screen would compare to the big stories inside my books.

As my love of books continued I read to entertain myself and escape a hectic life as a military wife and mother of seven.

Books also provided me with an education. I had left school early and as the children grew I had to continue learning to keep up.

As I continued to read I couldn't turn loose of some books. I became a collector of sorts, surrounding myself with the words I loved and creating a comforting book environment in my home.

The habit of reading was good for me but caused other reactions in the family. It kept me sane in a chaotic world and took me away mentally from those around me; you might have to ask me twice for attention if I was into a good book.

I read through thirty-six years of marriage, seeing my children off to lives of their own and through a divorce. My home-library, that had included fiction,

history and gardening books, now included a shelf of self-help books.

In 1990 I paid two dollars for a box of books at the Roscoe Library. The library, located in New York's Catskill Mountains, was having a book yard sale and toward the end of the day books were boxed to get rid of as many as possible. Inside the box I purchased was a small book that had not sold for the price of thirty five cents. It had been lumped together with other books, and marked as a box-lot.

After I made my purchase, and after discarding all but the small book, I made my way from the village of Roscoe back up the mountain to my Shandelee farmhouse.

After parking my truck, and carrying in a load of firewood, I made a fire in the fireplace and put on the teakettle. With the fire going, and the tea brewing, I sat down with my purchase.

Even then the little book was fragile. The edges showed wear and the pages were yellowed. However, the binding was good and there was no "old book"

smell. Never-the-less, I was careful as I turned the first page and began to read.

Who knows what our connection is with certain books but, after reading the first chapter, I am certain this book had called my name at the yard sale. I felt as I opened the cover and turned page after page I was entering a world I had been to before.

As I sat reading, and drinking hot tea before the fire, I felt comforted by everything around me. My home was furnished to my eclectic taste with my favorite pieces and it was filled with colors that made me happy. I remember the tea was plain orange pekoe, with a little sugar and milk added, and I had lemon tea biscuits to eat. The fire warmed my body, the tea and biscuits filled my belly and I experienced a sense of peace.

As I read the words of Frances Duncan, written so many years ago, I felt, though she was of another time, she was as contemporary as any writer I had ever read. As the evening wore on I couldn't put the book down. I needed to go to bed so I banked the fire, turned off the lights and, carrying my little book, went up the stairs.

When I was ready for bed I propped myself up to read. I continued reading until late in the night and didn't stop until I had I finished the book. I slept sound that night.

A few days later I re-read the book and over the last nineteen years I have read it many times, each time with as much delight as the first time.

With each reading I further connected with the main character. I understood where she was when the story began and as the story unfolds I continued to understand how a small thing can impact your life. I too had been sick from overwork and a garden had been the pivot point to my recovery.

So, after checking the copyright laws, and at my own expense, I bring you the words of Frances Duncan, complete and unabridged. I hope you enjoy her words and story as much as I continue to.

Yours truly,
Patricia Lanza,
June 19, 2007
My Garden Doctor

Chapter One

I doubt if ever a new-winged butterfly drying moist, uncertain, exquisite wings in the first sunshine that ever it felt, had more wonder at a new-found world or found it harder or stranger to look back to the old life in the chrysalis. It's so wonderful a thing—the mere being alive!

I had been ill, you must know, this long time—two or three years, it was. Not dangerously ill—that might have been exciting—but sunk in that spiritual and bodily quagmire, the Slough of Despond which we used to call "nervous prostration". Now it is known by a dozen imposing names—psychasthenia, neurasthenia, hypochondria, and the rest, according, I suppose, as to whether the quagmire has really gripped you, or whether you're sitting down on the edge of it and won't try to get up.

There are dozens of ways of reaching it. Too much work will bring you there, or too little; too much pleasure, or none at all. My road was overwork, or, rather, work with no admixture of play—the result, I suppose, of owning a New England conscience.

To my mind, that diseased and enlarged type of conscience known as New England is responsible for more neurasthenia, more ills of the body and mind, than any other one thing. Leave New England and go South, less and less grow the number of nerve-wrecks; leave it and go West, the same diminution may be observed. The fact is not without significance.

It is not a real conscience, either—this New England organ—but a changeling, an untoward brat born of decadent Puritanism and an unquiet digestion, yet it wears the front of Minerva and carries the aegis of Jove. It usurps the mastery of your spirit and directs your life. It says to any joyous emotion, "Lie down, sir!" Whenever you think of amusing yourself, up pops Conscience like a Jack-in-the-box and says, "Don't!" Does a pleasure present itself. Straight the conscience exhibits an unpleasing duty to be preformed in its stead. Atlas must have had a New England conscience or he never would have tried to carry the world on his shoulders.

The New England conscience produces the scholar, the divine, the man of research, the jurist, the lawyer, the financier, the philanthropist, and the social-uplifter; especially does it give us teachers in abundance, but never does it produce the artist, the creator, the man who has joy in his work. These have either escaped the microbe, or, if born with it, have isolated it or counteracted it in some way; some have even "gone to the bad" to get rid of it; but this latter course is more drastic than is necessary.

The New England Conscience insures you a colorless existence of useful work with the joy of life carefully excluded; it detects duties where the normal person would see never a one; it makes you do work that properly belongs to others, pick up burdens that were never designed for your carrying, while their lawful bearers lie down in the road. It makes you spend your life as a rigid economist, would have you spend your money-so that you get no enjoyment whatever from it.

That was what mine did for me.

And then this conscience leaves you, as mine left me, stranded, at seven or eight and twenty with the best days of life gone by. Nothing much done, nothing ahead; a burden to long-suffering relatives.

And then, in this extremity, does the conscience come to your rescue? Does it brace you with the conviction that you've acted a noble part? Does it fortify you as it fortified martyrs at the stake?

Not at all.

Precisely as a mean playmate who has gotten you into a scrape sneaks off and leaves you to take the punishment, so does this conscience sneak off and leave you to Mother Nature.

And Mother Nature is in no complaisant mood.

You can neither eat nor sleep nor read nor talk; you can just listen while she pounds your life to you clearly, forcibly, coldly.

She tells you that you've been a fool, a plain fool—
that the situation was wholly unnecessary. She tells you
this; she repeats it; she dins it into your ears; rubs it
in day after day, week after week, month after month,
into every nerve and muscle, with the thoroughness and
energy of an osteopath.

And never a word in your defense says the cowardly
conscience. It slinks off and disclaims responsibilities,
while in a secluded chamber, shut off from the life to
which you thought you were essential and find you aren't,
Mother Nature has her "innings". She explains things to
you in something this fashion—a catechism to which
she supplies both questions and answers. The questions
vary to suit the case, but their import is the same:

"Got your degree?"

"Much good it will do you here on your back."

"Sent your brother through college?"

"Quite as well for him—better—to have worked his
way."

"Provided handsomely for your family?"

"Very bright! Don't you know that straightened

circumstances don't hurt children in the least, so they have a father and mother intact?"

"Good motives?"

"The path to Neurasthenia has quite as many good intentions in its pavement as the path to Hell. Lac of intelligence is what you've shown. You've overdrawn your account. You're bankrupt physically and nervously. You must pay."

"Pay what?" you ask feebly.

"Three or four years—perhaps your whole life", says Madame Nature carelessly. "How should I know? You'll never be much good again."

This and much more from Madame Nature.

. . . .

After a while it was not so bad. Life hadn't been so wildly exciting that I felt I was missing much. There were books. There are foolish and satisfactory ways of amusing yourself in your head—as foolish and satisfactory as the game of tit-tat-toe to one's infancy. Then there are symptoms. There's your heart and your stomach and your head, whether you slept or didn't—

these are of engrossing interest to yourself, though they pall sometimes on your family. As for what happens outside—you care not at all, no more than a clam cares about mountain scenery. All you want is to be let alone.

I should have been there yet, in the quagmire, if it hadn't been for the new nurse. My chance came with her.

It had been rather a relief when Miss Watkins went. She was a good enough nurse, I suppose, as nurses go, but her nose worried me—it was too thick at the end; she had lips that closed tightly when she didn't talk, but she talked most of the time. She used to tell me all she could think of about the hospital—how they "laid out" people, and matter of like interest with vivid and abundant detail. She wouldn't let me alone. She kept digging into my sandbank—metaphorically, of course, but it worried me.

The new nurse was different. I liked her from the first. She was tall and strong and dark and she had a very quiet face. Her profile was beautiful; I think she didn't know that. She had a chin like Rossetti's Blessed

Damozel, but there the resemblance stopped, for the nurse wore eyeglasses, and the dark hair that ought to have been parted and worn in a knot at the back of her neck was put up in a pompadour, and her little white nurse's cap was frilled, which suited her no better than It would have suited the Rossettti lady. But these were matters that might be mended. "Miss Clarke" she was; I called her "Clarky".

Chapter Two

It was about three weeks after Clarky came to me that I began to sit up. A nuisance, but the doctor insisted. So for a half hour a day I was put in the big chair by the window, tucked in with pillows and rugs, and I had the tedious pleasure of looking at the blank February sky above and the blank expressionless yards below, that from the window of our "third-story-back" constituted our prospect. Back to back, were the yards, a double row of brown, wooden compartments, all precisely the same, and for all the world like the pasteboard compartment-box a grocer fills with eggs. Only these were empty.

"Who's the round old gentleman in the next yard?" asked Clarky one day.

I leaned toward the window. She had just given me my nourishment, some sort of eggy stuff, and stood by the other window waiting until I had finished.

"That's the Kreisler's yard." I explained, "it must be their Uncle Hermann." Clarky took the glass and the little plate and went out, leaving me looking down at Uncle Hermann. A round, fat, little man he was and he seemed fussing with a brown mass of vines on the fence. I watched him absently, just as I watched the Thomson's cat walk carefully along the fence top, deftly eluding the cat-teasers and going where she would. Uncle Hermann still kept poking at the fence; presently I noticed that branches were beginning to form a pile on the bare grass-plot beside him. Then, as I watched, the fence emerged from the brown mass at one side, and against it, plainly in view, was a single branch trained upward.

"Clarky," I said, as I heard the door opened, "give me the opera-glasses, please, top drawer, chiffonier, right-hand side. " I want to see what Uncle Hermann is doing."

I focused the glasses on the yard below. Now I could see. He was clipping with scissors and every now and then feeling in a pocket for a bit of something that he tacked to the fence with a hammer he kept in the other pocket, while on the fence was beginning to appear a design of branches, springing from a single stem, branching like the seven-golden-candlestick I remembered seeing in a Sunday-school quarterly of my youth.

"What's he doing?" I asked.

Clarky took the glasses, screwed them a bit—she is near-sighted—watched attentively a moment:

"He's pruning the roses, Miss Caroline, and he's pruning them in good old German style. He's going to have a handsome espalier arrangement on that fence".

"Why does he prune them?" I asked.

"They'll bloom better".

"But why now? Nobody cuts his bushes until May".

Clarky smiled, "Uncle Hermann knows what he's about. Now's the time for roses. Later, the vines would bleed, now the cuts will heal before the sap runs, not a bit of vitality will be lost."

"How did you know all that?", I asked, when she had put me back into bed.

Clarky laughed. "My mother was English," she said; "I used to help her prune the roses when I was a little girl. I've seen her do just exactly what Uncle Hermann's been doing."

"Tell me about it."

"About what?" She folded the rugs, put the pillows back on the couch, and was moving about the room putting one thing and another in its place.

"You know—about pruning the roses. Sit down in the big chair and tell me."

She sat down in the big chair, took off her eyeglasses, pushed back the dark hair, looked out across the little yards and ever so far beyond.

"It was 'way up in Massachusetts that we lived," she began, "up near the edge of Vermont, but my mother was English and she would have her roses. All up on one side of the house they were, on a lattice—Sweet Brier, Baltimore Belle and the Seven Sisters were climbing roses. There was a tangle of old cinnamon roses below

the house; then we had a York and Lancaster by the front door, and a bed with Jacqueminots and Boursaults, Maiden's Blush and a beautiful old Damask, Moss roses we had too. It would be a day like this that my mother would take—the first warm day, only it would be in early March—you know, and the season's a bit later. I would have on an old frock and big gloves and she would let me cut the easiest branches."

"First the dead wood must come out. Then the weak shoots—I used to cut out those. 'To him that hath shall be given,' she used to quote as she pointed out the big, strong shoots that must be cut and showed me the little ones that I could cut, 'it's gardening, and Scripture, and I believe it's finance also.' But the more artistic business such as we saw Uncle Hermann doing—that she always did herself. My work was to stand by and hold the tacks and hammer and the little strips of cloth. Afterward, I would pull away the cut branches, rake them into a pile, and then we'd burn them together—a glorious bonfire we'd have! I can smell it yet—the scent of the burning wood in the clean March air! The air has come off the snow banks, and you know it. But it would be warm sunshine, quite warm by our old house, even when there's snow up under the big hemlocks——-"

"Then?"I questioned, for Clarky had stopped.

"Then we'd sit down on the doorstep a bit and rest after working, and look off at the hills. That is my mother would look off at the hills, but I would poke in the brown grass beside us to find the hard little pints of crocuses coming up. My mother used to say they were wrong in changing the calendar—it was then the year began, not January."

"But what did you see?" I begged.

"From the doorstep? Oh, we looked over the tops of orchard trees, then rough, broken pasture land; then over the meadows and river to a little town. We could see the roofs and the smoke rising; hills that were thickly wooded behind it; then the blue of distant ranges beyond and beyond! There would be hardly a sign of life in the trees now, but just a little later there's the faintest haze over them, first at the edge of the pasture land. You think it's the atmosphere, it isn't, it's the coming alive!

Oh, and then you watch or you miss something! The branches are dark and distinct—it's only in the very tips, where the twigs are so fine you can't see them, that there's life. There's a moment when the tips of big oaks in the distance have an aureole of pale gold; there's just one moment when the black birch has the color of an amethyst——Did you never see it?" she demanded.

"Never," I said. "I'm not a poet, Clarky, besides I've only been to the country in summers—July and August—and then to hotels."

Clarky was silent a moment, then—

"You've something to live for, Miss Caroline," she said quietly, "I'd get well, if I were you, just for that."

Chapter Three

After this day, we watched Uncle Hermann—that is I watched him. After he had the roses done to his taste, he began lifting with a fork something that was on the narrow little side-beds and making piles of brown stuff in the walks. Then he would get down on his knees on the bit of old carpet he had brought with him to lay on the chilly flagging of the walk, and poke in the beds.

"He has a lot of young things coming up there, I'm sure." Said Clarky. "He can't dig with a spade—he might hurt them—he has some sort of funny little old weeding fork, and he's loosening the soil."

"How does he know where they are?"

"Oh, he'll know where everything is: you always do." She explained.

"What do you think he has there?" I asked.

"It's his bulbs he's looking for—winter aconites, snowdrops, scilla; they'll be showing—perhaps the tips of daffodils. Then he wants to know if anything's been hurt. Hollyhocks might have rotted, you know. Besides, he might find a pansy in bloom."

"He might give it to me if he does," I grumbled.

But Uncle Hermann had no idea how interesting he was.

Toward the end of March we had day after day of rain.

I sat by the window my allotted time, looked down at the yards among which Uncle Hermann's golden-candlestick arrangement of roses shown resplendent, and I did some thinking.

Then came the sunshine.

"Uncle Hermann will be gardening to-day, surely," said my nurse.

"Clarky," I replied, "I don't want to watch Uncle

Hermann, I want to talk. Have you any sporting blood in you? Are you good for something reckless?"

Clarky laid down the thick steamer-rug—she was placing the pillows for me in the chair. "Very reckless?" she asked.

"Very. Listen. There's a little old house up in your country that belongs to me. My grandmother lived in it years and years ago. There's no one in it now, I believe. I was there once when I was a little girl, but all I remember is an apple tree that you could climb, some yellow lilies along by the stone wall, a pasture that had a brook in it—there are hills, I know. It's in Enderby—that's farther north than you are —New Hampshire. Will you go up there with me, just you and I? Will you go next week? I want to see the trees come alive? I want to poke in a garden-bed like Uncle Hermann! I want to see those dear little things come up, and loosen the soil for them! I want to make a gorgeous seven-golden-candlestick thing out of a climbing rose? But there mayn't be one there—still we can plant it! Will you come?"

Clarky looked at me a moment, "You haven't walked yet," she began slowly.

"Only to the big chair," I said, "but I'm going to! Besides, I could lie down on a rug or a mattress and poke in a garden-bed beautifully!"

Clarky considered, scanning me closely.

"It's time for your eggnog," she said at last, by way of answer, and went to fetch it.

It was a full half hour that Clarky kept me hung up in the air waiting for the eggnog and the answer.

At last she came.

"Well, I asked, "Will you come?"

We'll have to find out if it's possible, I mean, if the place is possible," she began. "I've been telephoning. Mrs. Prittchard will take care of you for a few days," repeated my nurse, "and if your willing, I'll go up to the little place in New Hampshire and find out if the thing's practicable."

"Good for you, Clarky!"

"You must not count on it too much, Miss Caroline," she said. "The roof of the house may leak. There may be water in the cellar and typhoid in the well, but I spoke with Doctor Brandon about it. He thinks a change would help you and that there's no possible harm in finding out what it's like. But that will take two or three days."

"Take a week, if you like, "I said, "but don't find any lions in the way! If you do, stop and shoo them off! I'll plan the garden while you're gone, and do penance for my sins with Aunt Cassandra."

"There's no harm in planning a garden," began Miss Clark.

"Oh, I'm going to," I assured her. "I've sent for some catalogues already. Maybe I'll get a garden book or two."

"Don't," she said, "the less you know, the more cheerfully you can plan!"

"You go on up to New Hampshire, Clarky! When you're back we'll talk it over. I won't order any plants till you come back!"

So Clarky left me to Aunt Cassandra and the catalogues. I confess I found the catalogues the better company of the two.

Chapter Four

I had a beatific time with the catalogues. They came the morning after Clarky left. I had tried my best to remember how the ground lay about the little house in the hill country, but it was no use. All I could remember was a haymow in the barn; an apple tree that stood on a steep slope; a swing in the tree, and when you swung out you went up into the branches and high—fearfully, beautifully high above the ground; and yellow lilies by a stone wall. Once I had fallen from the wall into the lilies, which fixed both in my mind. None of these items was of much help in deciding where I'd put the garden, so I quit this mental research and turned my attention to what I'd put in it.

Two catalogues I had. First I read them all through and looked at the pictures, just as if I were a child and they were fairy-books. They were, of a kind, for you put a seed or a bulb in the ground and out comes a fairy princess! It's quite as wonderful an idea as Aladdin and the Lamp, and I was to be Aladdin!

Then I came down to practicalities.

I took a little note-book and made a "visiting list." There were two reasons for doing this. First, I wanted to; secondly, I knew that if Aunt Cassandra came in and saw me busy with a pencil, she might conclude that I was profitably employed and not "lonesome" and that she needn't come and talk to me, which would be a gain.

On this "visiting list" I wrote down the names of all the flowers and bulbs and shrubs I liked best. I put down the ones I knew and the ones I didn't know, but thought I'd like to know. Of course, I liked the names—those sonorous, slow-syllabled Latin names—of some the description was alluring. I liked the sound of Lilium

PATRICIA LANZA
auratum, Helenium maginficum, Lychnis, Monarda, Enothera, Arabis, and Bellis perennis; I liked the sound of Campanula. I think there's a bee in Pippa Passes that had something to do with a campanula—

"Where he hid, you could only guess.

"By some campanula chalice set a-swing"—so, I think the line runs. A bee might do the same in my garden—anyway he should have opportunity. Then there were Sea Lavender and Spring Adonis—a lovely thing surely!

Next came less poetic reasons. I put down Gaillardia, because I knew and liked the Carolina Gaillards. Aconitum Napellus I had known only as a medicine and thought it but fair to meet it under another guise. Digitalis, however, I excluded—I'd taken too much of it! It could be as handsome as it liked, but I wouldn't have it in the garden. Irisis and roses, oh, ever so many roses! These seemed more personal because most of them had Christian names instead of Latin ones. It sounded pleasantly sociable to invite to my garden Ulrich Brunner, Frau Karl Drushki and Papa Gontier

and Lady Gay, who sounded very cheerful; I chose Mme,
Casimire-Perier, a lilac, because I had seen her on the
stage and was interested to discover how she'd appear
horticulturally. (Later, I may say, I learned to select
plants more intelligently, but this is the way I selected
them then, and a fine time I had doing it!) Beside the
names, I put down color and blossom time and "sun"
or "shade," whichever it preferred. Then I "located", as
the detectives say, a box of colored pencils I once had,
and I underlined each name with a pencil mark as near
the color described as I could hit. "Rosy purple, " for
instance; the catalogue seemed very fond of that, and
what on earth is it? "Rosy red flushed with salmon" was
another poser. But I finished my little note-book and it
looked highly interesting, albeit somewhat childlike.

Next I made a half dozen little books out of note-
paper doubled over once with a pin for binding and
named them April, May, June, July, August, September;
and I took my "visiting list" and entered each plant
where it belonged; some figured in two or three books.
I suppose this sounds silly, but there's nothing more

tiresome when you're ill than trying to find what you want among loose papers. Besides, what I did later sounds sillier to any one who hasn't been a neurasthenie and doesn't know that in such cases one may exhibit the artlessness of childhood and the foolishness of senility, but his actions do not reflect the judgment and hard sense of middle life.

I know a brilliant man of letters who solaced himself during a convalescence by taking a fishing-rod and "casting" from his position in bed. Hooking any interesting object within reach and hauling it in. Beside this, I hold my occupation was intellectual.

I made another book of note-paper and colored the cover bright yellow. (To return to my kindergarten employments.) That was for sunshine. I cut the inner leaves so that they opened index fashion and gave a few leaves to each month. Then I took my visiting list and wrote in its proper section, first the plants that must have sun; then, with a division line between, those catholic ones that relish either sun or shade. I colored these properly, for that was half the fun.

Next I made another book with the cover half green and half yellow, like the garb of the Pied Piper—that was for partial shade; and yet another book, all green, in which were shade-loving plants, arranged as in the yellow book. Then I laid back on my pillows and rested from my labors, looked at my little books and felt proud and satisfied. Not yet had I planned my gardens, but it was something to have the dramatis personae selected. The scenes could be arranged later.

Chapter Five

At last Clarky came back. I didn't see her until she entered my room in her nurse's uniform, just as if nothing had happened. But she looked cheerful.

I hate that barrack-discipline that makes a nurse stop and change her dress when you are dying to find out something.

"Tell me everything about it," I demanded.

She laughed. "I'm not going to tell you a thing—except this. It's possible."

"Possible!" I exclaimed. "You mean we can do it?"

She nodded.

"Good for you, Clarky! When? Next week?"

She laughed. "There's snow up there yet. In four weeks, I should think—end of April—perhaps."

"Four weeks!" I exclaimed, "What a horribly long time! Never mind. Tell me all about everything!"

"There's nothing to tell," she answered. "You'll see it all."

"But what did you do?" I persisted.

"Well, I drove up to your little house in a sleigh with a tall youth who had bad teeth and whose name was Alonzo Kendall. Your house is off the highway and not easy to reach. The road hadn't been traveled at all. It was what Alonzo called 'bad going'. The snow was hard on top and thawed beneath. You don't know whether the horse's foot is going to stay on top or sink a foot or two. The horse doesn't know either."

"How disconcerting for him! What else besides Alonzo and the 'bad going'?"

"Mrs. Tarbox. We stopped at her house for the keys. She lives at the foot of your hill."

"Who's she?"

"Alonzo's aunt, round and cheerful and talkative.

She will clean the house, have fires lighted, and dinner for us when we arrive. Alonzo will haul some wood and have firewood cut in the woodshed. He promised to clean the spring, too. I went up the hill with him and looked at it—waded through snow—it's deep by the spring that's in a hollow under a big maple up the hill. Mrs. Tarbox lent me her rubber boots."

"Oh, I remember!" I exclaimed, "there's a great stone over half of it, boards over the rest, and you can peek through and see the water."

"That's it," said Clarky.

"And apple trees? Are there apple trees?"

"Yes."

"And a barn?"

"Yes."

"And a lilac bush?"

"And a good place for a garden?"

"Plenty of places for a garden."

I drew a breath of relief.

"Now, what's the house like?"

"It's a little, old, story-and-a-half farmhouse, just

like hundreds of others in New Hampshire."

"Pretty?"

"It could be pretty. There is good paneling in the living-room. There are fireplaces, but they've been boarded up. The paper is in tatters, and the woodwork is painted pink."

"Pink,", repeated Clarky firmly—"a depressing pink with drab panels. The McIntyre's farmer was the last one who lived there. He must have liked pink. It's in the kitchen, too. And the kitchen walls are papered with hideous paper. There's a big fireplace, but it is boarded over."

"Upstairs?"

"You open a door in the kitchen and the stairs go up from there into an unfinished attic, but in it are two rooms finished off."

"Where am I to be?"

I think you'd be best downstairs, Miss Caroline. There's a big sunny room downstairs across the hall from the living-room. It would be easy for you to get outdoors and back again, and there's a little room

behind it that I could have."

"But supplies, Clarky? What about manna or quail for wilderness? Or will Alonzo act the Raven to our Elijah?"

"I've ordered a telephone put in. The grocer at Enderby Centre will send out twice a week. Mrs. Tarbox will cook for us—perhaps. She said she'd 'see about it'. I'll contrive that we don't starve. Well, do you like it?" she asked, for I was staring dumbly at her.

"Like it!" I cried. "It's the most exciting thing that's ever happened to me! It's the first time I ever went away to do exactly what I wanted. And such a joke to do it when I'm limp!"

"Clarky, tell me——" then I stopped, suddenly remembering that she must be tired; so for ages— and exactly five minutes by the clock—I asked no questions. I just laid there and thought about Alonzo and the "bad going," and the little house up on the snow-covered hillside, with the eaves dripping in the warm March noon.

Then I began again—"Clarky, tell me one more

thing. What shall I see from my window?"

She thought a moment.

"From your front windows," she said slowly, "you look down a long slope to the break in the fence where the gate use to be. On one side a wide stretch— mowing land. I suppose it is—on the other, the edge of the woodland. Then you look over the tops of pines and birches to the hills beyond, and a mountain in the distance, blue, a gentian blue, it is now. It's a lovely outlook. From your side windows you can look right into the woods; the little house is almost at the edge of the forest."

"That's like the fairy-books," I said, "the little cottages where nice things happen are always at the edge of the forest. Snow-white and Rose-red lived there, I believe. The dwarfs would be in the woods. And no house within sight?"

"None. There's a little red house at the foot of the hill, but you can't see that."

"The witch lives there, of course."

"Mrs. Tarbox lives there," corrected Clarky.

"The pasture; did you see the pasture?"

She shook her head.

"Only the edge, when I climbed the fence to look at the spring."

Are there bulbs and things to come up in the garden-beds, like Uncle Hermann's?"

"I can't tell. There was snow on the ground (I drove out in the sleigh, you know), but the snow was melting in the sunshine and the water dripping from the roof—I saw one rosebush near the house, but it was a rather forlorn one."

"What's the color of the house?"

"White, it was once. It's gray now, and the woodshed's dropping off. The biggest gray squirrel I ever saw lives in your woodshed."

"And you don't know what's to come up near the house?" I said disappointedly.

"No, I don't, but even if there's nothing near the house, there will be lovely things in the woods."

"Will there?" I said. "What things?"

"Bloodroot. Our hillsides were full of that. It's the

most exquisite white. You will find it under the trees showing above the dead brown leaves, it looks like snow only so wonderfully alive. Then you'll find the rue anemone and the wood anemone, Dutchmans's breeches, and that fragile, lovely little star-flower— the woods are full of that. We'll find them all in your wood."

"Do you think so?" I asked

"Surely. And there will be saxifrange on the rocks and bluets in your pasture—great patches of them— deep blue in the shadow, and almost white where they lie in the sun all day."

"And you think I can really go?"

"I'm sure of it," she said.

Then she left me. I think I cried a bit; I was absurdly weak yet absurdly happy over it.

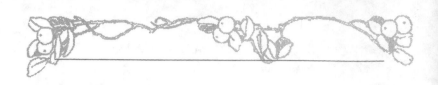

Chapter Six

I was quite ill again for a week or more after that. I suppose it was the excitement; perhaps it was my wild orgy of horticultural industry, but neither Clarky nor I changed our plans for a moment. When I couldn't talk or listen or plan, I laid still and thought about the patches of bluets in the starved pasture grass, and of bloodroot opening white and wonderful above the dead brown leaves.

All this time next door, Uncle Hermann went happily on with his gardening. He was planting now, so Clarky said—I couldn't sit up to watch him—and his crocuses were in bloom, and his daffodils showing fine green stalks. I didn't much care to see them, I wanted to see the little things come up in my own garden.

Over and over again I planned it. Now I would put hollyhocks by the little house—great tall ones that could look in the windows, and I made a path and had daffodils on each side in rows. I had roses; climbing roses—over the door; then I sat on the doorstep and admired the roses. Then I changed it and I put the hollyhocks by the path and the daffodils under the windows. I trained the roses against the house, to go under and around the windows. All this was in my mind's eye, of course. When you're ill you learn to amuse yourself in your head until the make-believe is almost as good as the actual.

I didn't order anything yet—that is, not any plants—but I did have some seed packets. Clarky took my visiting list and ordered seeds of all the annuals I had put down there.

On the days when I couldn't sit up, I used to lie and finger the packets; spread them out on the counterpane. Centuaurea, Mignonette, Marigolds, Shirley Poppies, Coreopsis—all the old one I knew and some new ones

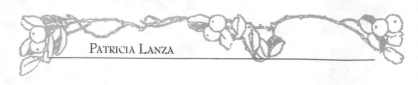

I didn't (such as Arctotis grandis which I had ordered because it sounds impressive). I read the directions on the packets which seemed all alike, "Sow out-of-doors when danger from frost is past, in a light rich soil," or else, "sow in boxes in the greenhouse in February." As if everyone had a greenhouse! In some of the packets I poked little holes and shook out a few seeds on the counterpane to look at them, and I wondered where was hidden the marvelous blue in the tiny silvery shuttlecocks that were to be cornflowers, where the gold lay in the little spurs that were marigolds. Most wonderful of all, was the infinitesimal grain of life that is a poppy seed. How can all that wealth of flower and stalk and bud be hidden in anything so marvelously small! Then I would look at the seeds, and wonder how they'd get on together in my garden and whether they'd like it.

As I held the seeds in my hand the old fairy-tales seemed very simple—I remembered that one of the Prince, who drew hundreds of yards of fine-spun linen from a nutshell and at last out sprang a beautiful maiden. Perfectly natural it seemed beside the miracle

of the poppy. The folk who made the fairy tales must have known well the miracles of the plants, I thought.

And so April passed. The last week came and the eve of our departure.

Chapter Seven

It was an adventure for Clarky. I saw her look to the priming of her nitro-glycerin syringe as a soldier looks to his gun and cartridge belt. Also, I caught her scrutinizing me with a keen, professional eye, and she took my respiration when she thought I didn't know it. But I did. And I made it as nice and even as I could.

I suppose the journey was something of a risk, but I didn't care in the least. When you've been ill long enough you come to consider your interior decorations and internal workings as wholly the affair of the doctor and the nurse; not your concern at all. They may do as they like with them. Even if there were a good chance of shuffling off the mortal coil in the proposed journey, I shouldn't have cared. And this wasn't morbidness or pessimism—nothing but pure indifference. You see, that in a long illness, so many of one's root-connections have been cut already, that whether it's transplanting, or complete grubbing up matters little. The real wrench was in the first cutting of the roots.

Still, I realized that an exit during the trip would have been embarrassing professionally for Clarky. There was little danger of it, however. Was I not going to dig in a garden-bed and see the trees come alive? Besides, I might come alive myself, like those little plant bundles we have stowed carefully back in their box—who could tell?

Anyway, it was a gorgeous adventure! I felt as exultant as Columbus when at last, after all the tedious waiting, Queen Isabella equipped his squadron and sent him off for the unknown seas!

Clarky, I fancy, didn't feel much like Columbus on the deck of the Santa Maria. Spenser's Una would be nearer her state of mind—Una when she set out for the wilderness with the ass and the dwarf and the

bag of needments—courage mixed with trepidation. But Clarky had far more intelligence than Spenser's heroine, and so long as we had a telephone and supplies we should need to search for neither Red Cross Knight nor lion. So does the modern convenience deal hardly with Romance!

A slight touch of romance we had—a very prosaic form.

The morning of the day we left came a box addressed to me; a rough wooden packing box. They were about to open it downstairs, but Clarky had it brought up and opened it herself in my room. LIVE PLANTS, PERISHABLE, NO DELAY was on top in large, imperative letters.

I'm not fond of packing boxes; I hate to be hurried. Two months ago I'd have delayed all I pleased, and if the live plants wanted to perish, they could perish! Now, it was different. I was thinking of coming alive myself, and had a fellow feeling for the shut-up plants.

I made Clarky put the box on a chair beside me after she had ripped off the cover. It was real Bassanio's casket—meagre in promise, but full of possibilities. I leaned over and felt in the cool, damp, springy moss until I found a bundle. Wrapped closely in the moss it was and wound about with a string—packed like an Indian papoose. A wooden label was slipped under the string, on which was scrawled in pencil Viola tricolor, Trimardeau.

"What are they, Clarky?"

I showed her the bundle.

"Pansies," she said.

I searched again in the soft, cool packing—delightful it was to the fingers—and found another bundle, and another—six in all.

"Did you order them, Clarky?" I asked.

She shook her head.

"Does anyone downstairs know about them?"

"No."

"I wonder who had the intelligence—" I said to myself slowly after Clarky had gone. Then I picked up one of the little bundles again and opened it carefully, held up the stubby little plants with the long, brown,

sandy roots and looked at them.

"I like you—you queer, unpromising-looking little things!" I remarked to the papoose-like bundle. "I like you heaps better than if you were American Beauty roses! They're so insultingly healthy and prosperous. You don't look like much, but yet there's life in you. We'll go up to the county together, you and I. If you can grow and amount to something, perhaps I can."

Then I put it back in the box and looked again in the moss.

At last I found in the bottom of the box (it had been packed as the top, I suppose) an envelope stained with the damp of the parking. There was a card in it.

"Partial shade, rich soil, and individual attention. The long, dangling things are roots, Caroline, and should go in the ground."

I knew the writing, though I hadn't seen it for a long time—Richard Protheroe's. An odd fellow, but he had a lovely garden.

"Can't we take them with us, Clarky?" I asked when she came in from one of her brief visits. "People take a kitten or a pup in a basket; why not live plants?"

"Surely," she said. "I'll find a basket. We're traveling light."

We were indeed to travel light. Everything had been sent before. I didn't know much about that; it was Clarky's end. My room kept as quiet as a cloister, but I know bedding and cots were sent, blankets and warm clothes a-plenty, a hammock and a camp-kit. I wasn't even to dress properly, just a dark skirt and sweater over my night-dress, then a long cloak and a soft hat, for I hadn't yet been dressed and didn't want to get tired. We were to take the sleeper from the Grand Central; there was no change; I would waken in New Hampshire, that was all. Very neat and simple!

There's a deal of difference between traveling when you're ill, but yet a little responsible, and then being simply "toted", an irresponsible bulk with no more thought of what may happen than if you were a bale of cotton. Being in the bale-of-cotton state of mind, I rather liked crossing the city at night, the rapid blurring of lights, the swift-moving motor; I liked it when we crossed the bridge, where below us lay the river, a strip of darkness flecked with moving lights—spanned by fairy-like arches of brilliance—on either side of which rose great dim bulks like giant castles, the lights blazing from innumerable windows. I liked the flashing of the electric signs where petticoats or the charms of chewing gum were blazoned with a startling distinctness that would have answered for a notice of the Day of Judgment. I didn't mind the Grand Central, nor the crowds that were so close to the wheel chair. It felt like going through a picture-book. I was no more a part of it than that. Only the pages turned so rapidly!

Then suddenly, the stuffy dimness of the compartment and every one out but Clarky and me.

"Well, do you like it?" she asked, after she had made me comfortable.

"Yes," I said, but my head was going around like the wheels of the wheel chair, and the people still kept going by, and my heart was "chugging" like a just-cranked automobile. So, being an accomplished invalid, I took out Wordsworth and began to read. In my head, of course. If you've been ill long enough, you learn to "turn on" verse or prose in your head, set it going as if it were a mechanical toy, and the immortal William W., as any neurasthenic knows, is the prince of sedatives, calm and placid with the large placidity of a cow content in a succulent pasture. So I "turned on" the Prelude—

> " *In what vale*
> *Shall be my harbour? Underneath what grove*
> *Shall I take up my home? And what clear stream*
> *Shall with its murmur lull me into rest?*
> *The earth is all before me. With a heart*
> *Joyous, not scared of its own liberty—* "

It ran along like the brook in my pasture, so the stuffiness was forgotten, and the loveliness-to-be was again present, and on the viewless wings of poesy, as Keats has it, I went up to the country far ahead of the train. A most convenient method. As for Clarky, she leaned back comfortably in her corner, snapped on the electric light, and opened the Evening Screamer,

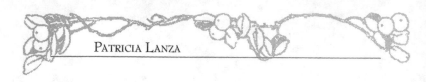
I suppose by way of a farewell to New York, and began to read.

It's Clarky's pompadour that makes her do that sort of thing, not her chin.

Chapter
Eight

The little house sat sunning itself on the warm, brown slope that April morning. As warm, it was as the sudden February day that first tempted out Uncle Hermann and set him a-gardening.

It was settled cozily into the great shoulder of a hill; and at it's back, oaks and beeches showed high above the low, broad roof; for from the pines of the hill a line of woodland reached down like a protecting arm, sheltering the little house from the rough Northeasters; and in this embrace it seemed very safe and warm—as content in the spring sunshine as a pussy-cat on a hearth. I think it would have purred if it could!

It did not seem in the least lonely; the great lilac bush at the corner had been the best of company; there were two friendly apple trees that stood a little down the slope and looked across the grassed-over road into its front windows. It was different with the great barns which stood to the south and farther up the hill; they looked gaunt and forsaken; but then, they had neither lilac bush nor apple trees to bear them company.

Instead of being exhausted, I had felt better as soon as we stepped out of the train at the Enderby Station. The air seemed deliciously sweet and clean and fresh; as sweet as a new-washed baby; it had been rain-washed and sunned, the scent of the fresh earth was in it, the pureness of the snows—as different from the makeshift stuff of the town as radiant sunlight from badly watered gas. The city air had simply sat heavily on top of my chest instead of going inside it; this went into every nook and cranny of my lungs, swept out all the horrid, dusty corners with the thoroughness of a vacuum cleaner, and much more inspiration.

Slowly we drove along the muddy road. Whenever

Alonzo skirted a puddle, the horses dropped cheerfully into a walk, which seemed their preferred gait. On one side were the brown meadows, fringed with low bushes where the river touched them, and across the river the little town—just as Clarky had said. On the other side of the road after we left the river and began to climb, the bank rose steeply, almost precipitously. The trees that overshadowed us grew high overhead; though the light growth of saplings I could see their strong roots gripping the rocks like giant tentacles. There were hundreds of tiny steams trickling out of the dripping hillside; they stole noiselessly in and out among the roots, slipped over the huge rocks, washing their faces for them. I could not see any flowers, but there were green ferns, as vividly green as if it were June, only they were pressed flat against the dead brown leaves, as if their blanket of snow had been drawn off so carefully they hadn't even been wakened by its removal.

It was a long, long climb, then we turned sharply into the merest lumber-track of a road. Level it was, and through gaps in the great pines we looked down on the meadows which seemed very far below, and saw the river winding among the blue hills. Then up a twisting narrow road where slender birches leaned and touched overhead and feathery young hemlocks came so close they almost brushed our muddy wheels with their pretty greenery, and the hard green ferns asleep against the bank were so close I could have touched them.

At every "thank-you-ma'am" the horses stopped to rest; the steady rhythmic creaking of the wagon ceased abruptly. Then the air was marvelously still; the clear tap-tapping of a distant woodpecker only made visible the silence. Once I heard a quick rustle and a sudden whirr of wings.

"A partridge," said Clarky.

A coppery chipmunk flashed along a fallen tree beside us, but he made no sound. Overhead, the topmost branches of one of the trees showed a faint flush, as if Madame Nature, her garment of snow removed, had found herself in the "altogether" and was blushing at her predicament.

Suddenly the trees left us; we passed through a

break in the fence, guarded by great butternut trees, and entered.

It was what Keats called a "wide quietness," these outspread acres over which the little house presided. The land, sloping softly to the south, closed in by the hill and the woods and the far-off fringe of dark trees, seemed as detached, as cut off from the rest of the world, as William Morris's "Hollow Hill." It was not an even slope; the strong, beautiful lines of the rough hill above were repeated lower in the scale—the brown acres lay in long fold, like softly falling draperies. The rain and the melting snows had given it a direction, like brush-strokes, so that one could see "the way the hills were put in," as painters say.

Soon I stopped thinking of the lines of the hill. I was looking at the little house, thinking we would never reach it—for I was beginning to be dreadfully tired. The distance that had looked so short suddenly became interminable.

"Well, Caroline," said a loud, cherry voice that, as we drove up to the door, smote on my ears like

an unexpected blasting explosion. "I was afraid you wasn't coming! Guess the nine-forty-five was late! Come right in and set down! 'Lonzo, you get out and hold Millie so's she won't start—she has a notion of going to the barn herself. Quite a sick spell you had, didn't you? Now catch right holt o'me. You want to set down on the doorstep? Well, all right! Jes' Miss Clark says. Glad to see you again, Miss Clark. An, you got her up here all right? Such a nice day's you had for comin'! Wasn't that splendid?"

I sank down limply on the doorstep, leaned against the post, looked vacantly up past the billowing expanse of white apron to a round rosy face let with gold rimmed spectacles that were bent on me. But I was as incapable of reply to the good Mrs. Tarbox's talk as the rocks were of saying anything to the streams that trickled over their faces.

"I ain't seen you, Caroline," she continued, "since you was a little girl. Must be twenty or twenty-five years ago, but I'd ha known you anywhere. You look jes' like Marsha Davenport, your mother's sister that was—she went into a decline"— she added in a whisper turning in Clarky's direction and looking significantly over her spectacless.

"Want I should take the trunk in, Aunt Cynthy?" spoke Alonzo, breaking in on the discourse. "They's other things down to the station. I got to make another trip."

"Yes, " Clarky answered him, "But I want you to help me a moment first."

Then she and Alonzo did something with a cot and pillows. The next thing I knew I was lying outstretched on something that was blissfully comfortable, looking up into the lilac bush, and Clarky was tucking rugs about my feet.

"You'll rest better here," she said, and left me.

I don't even remember anything more until she touched me on the shoulder.

"Eleven," she said. She had a cup of steaming bouillon in her hand.

I stared vacantly, first at her, then at the cup of bouillon, then up into the branches overhead, wondering how they came to be united in the same dream.

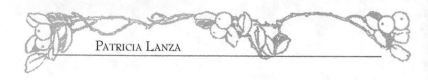

"Have we done it?" I asked, "or am I asleep?"

"We've done it," she answered "but it's time for your nourishment."

I stared a moment blankly, then I comprehended.

There's an inexorable regularity or orbit in a trained nurse that nothing can dislocate. It's like those dollar watches that go on ticking if you drop them from a roof or the brink of a precipice.

Chapter Nine

For two weeks I did nothing but be out-of-doors; sometimes my cot was set near the lilac bush where Clarky had put me the first day; sometimes she dragged it out to the old, grassed-over road, where I had the apple trees for company.

Meanwhile she did things to the house. I didn't much notice what, I only knew it kept getting more and more comfortable. I would catch the sound of a hammer in the house; then the big woodpecker on the apple tree would begin hammering, too, as if he were making fun of her.

Clarky loved a hammer and nails. I think she had as fine a time with her hammer as I had had with the catalogues. But regularly as a cuckoo pops out his clock at the stroke, out she would come at the tick of the hour. At ten with a glass of water; at eleven with nourishment; at twelve forty-five with tonic.

At one we would have a picnic. She would bring to the side of my cot a little table she had made of a packing-box-top, and we would have lunch together.

When the afternoon grew cool I was brought indoors and deposited on the living-room window seat. For Clarky put two cots together, end-to-end, under the living-room windows; these, covered with Navajo blankets, made our window-seat. She made a wainscoting of burlap and tacked it over the tattered paper, covering the worst. She struck hemlock branches in the top of it, and in the dusk and the firelight—the only time I was in the room, I found it charming. The only furniture we possessed was a square table and some roomy chairs.

Only people who have lived in furniture choked, bric-a-brac cluttered houses appreciate the utter rest of a state of furniturelessness. It's like Eden before the Snake suggested the necessity of being like other people. Nude the room might have been, but it was not naked in our eyes. I thought it perfect when the whole adornment was our wainscoting of hemlock branches and a great branch of budding maple in an old stone crock.

I hold Clarky's packing-box table—which was light enough and narrow enough to be lifted through the doorway and carried, with dinner on top, wherever we would be on the landscape,—the acme of achievement in modern furniture making.

Mrs. Tarbox didn't regard it in that light. She was really sorry for us! She hoped we could at least have lace curtains. I am sure she thought I was unsound mentally and that Clarky, in her actions, was humoring delusions that might be dangerous if opposed.

My room had funny, old fashioned wallpaper on it and a fat little round iron stove—"chunk stove," Mrs. Tarbox called it. It had short, wide-apart legs, and always reminded me of a stubby, enormously fat building— the little round draft at the front was his muzzle; the

stove-pipe, his tail; it was a cheerful, roaring little thing and excellent company. Clarky used to make a fire in it, at night and in the morning, when I was undressing and dressing.

During these days that I could only lie still, it was great fun watching Clarky. I had expected that the country would have a reviving effect upon me, but that it would transform her so speedily and completely, I never-dreamed. She would shed the brassbound stiffness of the professional nurse as quickly as a man kicks off shoes and throws off coat and vest when about to jump overboard for a rescue. She forgot her cap, she put her thick dark hair in a knot, sometimes in a heavy braid; she produced a pair of tortoise-shell full moons of spectacles, and wore them instead of the eyeglasses. She quit her uniform and substituted a short dark skirt and a man's canvas shooting-coat with pockets capacious enough to hold her beloved hammer and tacks and nails, and anything else she was minded to put in them. She made Alonzo bring her a saw from Enderby Centre and sundry other tools. She made a rough ladder herself, climbed it, and stuck a few shingles in the roof, for it leaked a bit, as we found one night when we had a heavy rain.

"I swan!" said Alonzo, when he saw her on the ladder, which expressed my feelings perfectly.

But all this time no garden! Try as we would, telephone as we would, not a soul could we get to dig it. Masculine Enderby Hollow had farming concerns of its own. Even Alonzo balked. He was working for Hiram Johnson, he told us, and couldn't get a single day off.

I didn't mind much. Clarky had stowed my pansies in a box with some soil she brought up in a pail from the ravine, so they were safe, and I was well content to have no gardening done while I was limply alternating between the outdoor cot and the bed inside. It might wait until I was "up and round", as Mrs. Tarbox said.

I was beginning to think of reviving, of climbing out of my hole like the woodchucks I used to watch. For at the top of each fold of the hill lived a woodchuck, and every afternoon I used to see them, each one sitting by the opening of his hole like a shopkeeper sitting at his door of a leisure afternoon.

One morning I tried it. It was brilliant sunshine. The woodpecker was hammering on the apple tree outside, Clarky was hammering inside. The nearest woodchuck, not content with sitting beside his hole, had come to a ledge of the old barn and was sitting there washing his face with his paw like a cat. I measured the distance, with my eye, from the cot to the long, narrow flower-bed next the house. It looked easy.

Carefully, laboriously I extracted myself from the tucked-up rugs. (Clarky had dressed me for warmth, rather than action) Woolen stockings I had on, woolen socks and moccasins, and a thick, dark blanket dressing-gown that trailed confoundedly. I tucked it up as well as I could, took a sofa pillow and sat down on it. I looked about me with the sense of pleased achievement that a toddler might feel who has escaped from his nurse. Then I scrutinized the ancient flower-bed.

Unpromising looking it was. It had been defined originally by a border of bricks that now straggled unevenly or lost themselves in the grass. The ground looked as hard-packed as that of an alleyway, and there

was a hollow filled with small pebbles, for the leader that should have been below the eaves was gone, and the dripping roof had worn away the soil.

I looked about for an implement; then I sat and thought. As a result, I drew a thick shell hairpin from my hair and with it I began to poke in the bed. In a second one prong broke off, then the other. After that I could work with it more conveniently.

Slowly, carefully, I pried up little chucks of soil, advancing the line of my excavations steadily, symmetrically, working with the systematic thoroughness of an archaeologist, digging among promising ruins. For a long time there was no reward, then, near the brick edge, about an inch below the surface, I found yellowish points like sprouting onions: The excavations grew intensely interesting; I found another and another of the hard young shoots. I covered them up and said nothing of my discovery, but when Clarky came out with our dinner I made her put her light-action table near the doorstep. She set her chair opposite and I sat on the doorstep leaning

against the frame, from which position I could admire my gardening.

Since then I've given less passionate admiration to more worthy examples of garden art. One is apt to give disproportionate value to his first efforts in an unknown art, just as a baby wins exorbitant praise from his adoring parents for taking a few steps, a feat which later they are able to view with complete unconcern.

Chapter Ten

"I can't go a-gardening with a fool thing like that flapping around my feet!" I protested as Clarky was helping me dress, and we had come to the blanket dressing-gown I had been wearing.

"Haven't I some Christian clothes—heathen ones would be more to the purpose, I daresay—but isn't there a hort skirt somewhere—and a sweater?"

Clarky grinned and went to find them for me.

Later when I was resting from the labor of dressing she brought me a bright new weeding-fork with a claw like a hen's foot—tense for scratching.

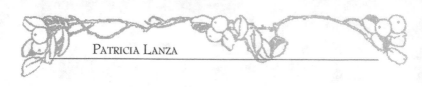

"You'll find that better than a hairpin." she said. "I've laid rugs all along on the grass in front of that bed you were scratching. Dig all you like, Miss Caroline, but lie down and rest the second you're tired. If you only dig alternate five minutes, you will put in thirty minutes' work in an hour!"

So I sallied forth, weeding-fork in hand, with a half-embarrassed feeling that Clarky regarded me as a child sent happily out to play in the sand with a bright new pail and shovel.

After I got to work I forgot the embarrassment of the pail-and-shovel idea—-the feeling of the archaeologist renewed itself; I worked steadily. Of course I could do but little at a time, and I kept at it day after day, until I had gone over every inch of the bed in front—under the living-room windows—and the one at the side. I straightened the wavering line of bricks that flopped hither and thither in a drunken fashion—a lovely green they were and moss covered. And I found lots of things! Mint there was, running everywhere; there were daffodils, some inside the line of bricks, some outside, evidently there had been a row; there were soft, mushy, whitish roots that Clarky said were hollyhocks; mats of clove pinks, and some other roots that she didn't know.

Which pleased me.

I get tired of having the role of Rollo fall invariably to me.

I put little circles of sticks around the roots I had found so that in digging we should not disturb them.

This was in the mornings.

In the afternoons I lay on the cot out of doors, rested, and watched the friendly woodchucks, wondering what labors they had completed that thus they sat at ease at the house door.(My little house had been empty so long, that the wild creatures were singularly unafraid. There was a darling little rabbit I used to see every morning under the windows; I don't know what he came for; he was brown and sleek and looked exactly like the toy rabbits you get for Easter and too small to be out in the world by himself. I hoped he hadn't lost his parents. Once, when I was dressing, a phoebe bird flew in the open window and instead of being in a panic at finding

himself enclosed, sat on the closet door that was ajar, chirped contentedly a minute, flew about inquiringly, then out of the window by which she had entered. And when I was sitting still for a moment's contemplation by my garden bed a young woodpecker flew suddenly from the lilac bush and landed on my shoulder. For half a second he and I stared at each other in astonishment: then he was gone to the apple tree and scrutinized me from there.)

By this time Clarky, having got the house more to our mind, began to concern herself with the gardening.

Oh, and lovely it was out of doors those days! The air was clear and sweet with the tang of the fresh earth in it and the snow that lingered still in the hollows; and the sky! It seemed to me I had forgotten completely what the sky was like—-the infinite depth and purity and the infinite unconcern of the slow-moving clouds: far up the hill we could pick out the trees as one and another woke to life—-here a rose-flushed maple, there a giant oak with the yellow of the spring sunshine caught in its hair; the young birches, a-tremble with life, stood out clear and delicate and lovely against the dark pines they chose for company; groups of slender little poplars that had slipped in from the woodland and were advancing toward the house were a charming yellow—paler than the oaks. And I saw the black birch—just as Clarky said it would be—amethyst—but in two days the color was gone and I couldn't find the tree among its darker fellows.

Clarky's first work when she set about gardening, was drastic. She took pruning shears and cut every sucker out of the lilac bush, until the branches and the shape of the bush stood distinct. Then she got her ladder, laid it against the bush and snipped off all that she could reach of the last year's blossoms.

"Now it feels better," she said.

Next she considered the flower bed—the one which ran from the doorstep to the lilac bush, under my windows. The ground sloped at the lilac bush end of the house, and the old flower- bed was so badly washed that not only figuratively, but literally, it was running downhill. Some two feet of the foundation showed, while on "my side" none at all.

Clarky looked at it. She said the best thing for that flower-bed would be a retaining-wall. She would make one.

By this time I was getting used to her large enterprises. Had she not just made a dining table with handsome legs of black birch, taking the saw to the woods, sawing there the legs, and bringing them home one by one? And with the aid of an iron rake wriggled the boards for the top of it down from high, impossible high, cross-beams in the barn?

So when she said she would make a retaining wall for my garden-bed, I simply said that would be nice; and watched the proceedings.

When the cart from the Center store came out on its biweekly visit with provisions, trailing behind it was a child's express wagon. The red-cheeked boy who drove the cart grinned as he unfastened it and led it up to Clarky.

I grinned, too.

But she didn't mind.

"Precisely what I wanted, thank you!" she said to him.

It would be far more convenient than a wheelbarrow, she explained. It would be useful if my legs crumpled under me when at some distance from the house—-I could be loaded on it and drawn home. We were not on Fifth Avenue nor Beacon Street.

I bribed the red-cheeked boy to dig my flower-bed, but he would only do part of it—just the front strip. Still, that was something. I smoothed it with my scracher and sowed things in it. Sweet alyssum on the edge; patches of poppies and cornflowers and mignonette, and morning glory next to the house. I know perfectly well I ought to have had it fertilized and enriched and all that sort of thing, but who could wait?

I helped a little with the "retaining-wall"—a "dry wall" Clarky called it. She said it must harmonize architecturally with the retaining wall below the house against which the roses grew. She brought down load after load of flat stones in the express wagon, getting

them from near the barn. I helped to place stones and we made a wall about a foot thick. It was two feet high at the lilac bush, diminishing until at the doorstep it was only a line of stones marking the bed. When Clarky's bed was filled with soil it would be on the same level as mine.

Gradually, as the wall rose, we filled it up with earth. This "we" is editorial. Clarky did the work, fetching pail after pail of muck from the ravine. Other things, too, she brought back from the ravine—Jack- in- the- pulpit, root and all, we set him under the lilac bush, just where the wall began, and he went on preaching contentedly, not minding in the least the change in the audience. She brought Herb Robert, hard little polypody ferns, tiny white violets and wood violets, baby hemlocks and maples. I planted these, sticking them into the chinks in the wall that we had stuffed with soil; they grew as if they had always been there. I thought it the loveliest kind of gardening.

We brought the wild gardening into the house also; violets and fringed polygolas, star flower and anemones, and one and another of the lovely little things I didn't know. Clarky didn't pick them, but took them up, brought them home on top of the pail of muck, and we put them in little pots in our living-room—not orthodox flowerpots, we hadn't any, but small wooded boxes and any little china or brass thing that would hold water and have room for the flower with a bit of earth besides.

When the flowers had passed, I set out the little plants in Clarky's garden. Much kinder it seemed than to pick and throw them away. We felt that for all our pleasure from them we had yet done them but slight injury.

The sweetest of all was the bloodroot; we had a round, pale green, Japanese dish filled with that on our table. Just at breakfast, the sunlight, coming through our small, old-fashioned windowpanes, touched the table; then I would move the little dish of bloodroot into it. One after one the dazzling white petals would open as we watched. I thought I had never seen anything so wonderful.

Chapter Eleven

The creaking of a wagon wakened me. I sat up to listen, sure I must be mistaken; no one ever came up our hill. The fox-sparrows in the roses were trilling their adorable little trill, three sweet notes, then the trill much higher. Usually it was they that wakened us. Sometimes there would be a dozen in the roses below the house. A thrush there was, too, over in the ravine, and another that answered him.

But the creaking of the wagon was unmistakable. It was coming nearer. Presently it came in sight. I saw it easily enough, for the old road had been close to the house; it was a lumber-wagon, with upright stakes around the platform; two horses, and a man driving—a man in corduroys with a canvas coat like Clarky's and a battered felt hat on the back of his head. The wagon passed, and from the sound, went up toward the hill and the pines.

We were at our early supper when it passed again. It was not yet dark; Mrs. Tarbox had just come in with a plate of hot biscuit; she set it down suddenly on the table and rushed to the window.

"My land!" she said. "Steve McLeod with a load of wood! Fifteenth of May an' he's just begun haulin'!" She dropped into a chair agast.

I didn't perceive the wickedness of going downhill with a load of wood of a May evening; I was only aware that it was a man on my hill, long sought, ardently desired. He might be useful.

"Do you think I could get him to dig my garden?" I asked eargerly.

Mrs. Tarbox eyed me severely. "My land!" she repeated. "Twouldn't do at all! That's Steve McLeod, Caroline!"

"Couldn't he dig my garden?" I asked again.

" I don't like you should have anything to do with him. Steve McLeod ain't all he should be," she said ominously.

"None of us is," I responded, "but what has he done?"

"Why," she said judicially, puckering her forehead, "I don't know as he's done anythin' special. It's what he ain't done. He ain't like other folks. And he's shif'less, terrible shif'less."

"He's always the las' one in town to get his seeds in. He's always doin' things at the wrong time—jes' always doin' things at the wrong time—jes' as you see now—he's haulin' wood and he'd ought to be plougin'; an when he'd ought to been haulin' wood, when they was aleddin', he was doin' suthin' else. Heavens knows what! He settin' up when he ought to be to bed, and to bed when he'd ought to be up and doin'. Mis Sile Holman, who lives jus' down the road from Steve, says he sets and reads dretful late—sometimes it's eleven, sometimes twelve o'clock 'fore he puts his light out. It really made her poorly worritin' about it an' settin' up to see how late it would be when Steve did put his light out. He ain't got good sense. He put his potatoes up the hill where the ground wa'n't good, and when Sile Holman asked why he did sech a fool thing he gave a dretful fool answer."

What was it?" I asked, interested.

"He said he liked the look of the mountain from there!"

"What's that got to do with potaters?" says Sile.

"Lots," says he, "I have to spend so much time hoein' the durn things I want suthin' to look at 'sides the potater patch while I'm a-doin' it."

"Folks think he ain't really responsible. He's got a brother, though, that's right smart—Alan McLeod. He's a big doctor to Boston.

"I ain't sayin's Steves bad, but he's foolish and he ain't like other folks. Still, I s'pose he might stop an' dig up a place for you, he's jes' getting' his ploughin' done an' have no time for nothin'."

"You'll ask him?" I said.

"Certainly I will, but he ain't much to have 'round.

I was drinking my early coffee the next morning when I saw Stephen McLeod's "team," as Mrs. Tarbox called it, coming slowly up the hill. (Clarky gave me my little cup of black coffee as early as six now, if I were awake—our schedule as been shoved forward—for I woke so much earlier and to square things had a long afternoon nap, like a baby.)

Just as the wagon passed, Mrs. Tarbox must have seen it, too, for I heard hasty steps across the kitchen floor, then the slam of the back door, then—

"Steve!"

"Who-a s-s-sh!" was the response. "Morning, Mrs. Tarbox."

Then a colloquay in which Mrs. Tarbox's strident tones alternated with a man's voice that was singularly low and musical, as much of a relief as the ripple of the water after a motor boat has let off its whistle.

Presently she came to my room. "He says he'd jes' lieves, Caroline, an' he wants to speak to you about it."

Clarky helped me on with my moccasins and put a long cloak over my wrapper, a scarf around my head and

I went out to the doorstep.

The man who was standing by his wagon came toward me, pulling off a dilapidated felt hat and baring a thick mass of bright brown hair. He was tall, rather loosely built, younger than I had thought; you couldn't see his mouth, the ragged beard hid it; his eyes were the eyes of a visionary. He reminded me a little of the "Apple-seed Johnny" of legend and history.

"You are Mr. Mcleod?" I asked.

"Yes, I am Stephen McLeod. Mrs. Tarbox says you wish to make a garden. Can I help you? I should like to."

He spoke hesitatingly, a little shyly, but the voice was singularly pleasant.

"I can't get anyone to dig it," I said.

"That I can do for you, " He answered; "where had you planned to put it?" I went with him to the little place back of the woodshed where evidently had been some planting before. He looked at it dubiously.

"Don't think it's very sightly," he said, "there's lots better garden-spots that this up here. You've got the

finest hill in all Enderby." He went over by the apple trees, and stood looking at the house.

"There's the place," he said, pointing just below the roses. "You've got the mountain to look at, 'stead of the side of the woodshed, and you'll see the trees beyond. When you've been weeding and stand up to straighten your back, you want something to look at,: he explained.

I thought of the potato field an smiled. "It is a good place," I said, "I can look down on it from my windows."

He was looking at the ground. "Have to plough it," he said; "sod's too tough for digging. I'll bring the plough to-morrow—'t won't take long, but I'll have to have it."

He did. It wasn't easy ploughing. There was one root of an elm that he kept striking. I liked to see the horses strain at the collars and go plunging over the rough land, pulling the plow though the stubborn soil. I liked to see the sods roll over, and the thick, black earth turn up.

I had no idea so much skill and deftness was necessary

in turning around and starting the furrow again. It was nearly ten when he un-hitched the horses from the plough, wiped his forehead which was curiously white, threw the extra whiffletree into the wagon, and began fastening the horses back into their old places.

"I have delayed you greatly, I'm afraid," I said. "Shall you be too late for loading the wood?"

He hesitated, looked at me keenly a moment, glanced nervously toward the house, then a sudden smile broke, he grinned like a boy, showing very white teeth, and his blue eyes laughed.

"The logging's an excuse," he said softly. "When it comes May, I just have to go to the woods, the trees are calling—I can't help it any more than those Hamelin children could help going after the Piper. Soon as the maples are out they fairly holler to me—I just take a week or so and say nothing to anybody. I have to go just like the bees go to that old orchard 'way up the hill; when it's in blossom, it calls them and they come. There's no one in Enderby Hollow knows what the May woods are like but me! All the men-folks are plowing and planting; all the women-folks are house cleaning. It's only the children that'd answer. They hear the woods calling plain enough; but them, they keep shut up in school 'cept Saturday, and they they get chores enough to keep them busy——- so they don't get too close to the Lord's miracle. And they teach them Easter and the Resurrection shut up indoor. Out of a Sunday-school quartly, when the bloodroot on the hillside is white as the garments of the Resurrection Angle, and every tree in the wood is a-tremble with the mystery of death transfigured into life!"

"They're blind and deaf, those peole down there!" he said passionately, pointing over toward the little town that lay below. "The only part of the Lord's miracle that they care about is that that helps' em feed their bodies— they never think of feeding their souls with it! 'Eyes have they but they see not, ears have they but they hear not, neither can they understand.' They drive the wild loveliness from the roadside as if it were pestilence. Do you think they'll see the gold in the streets of the New Jerusalem if they can't see the gold there?" he pointed to a great oak, leaning toward us from the ravine. "Do you think they could see the Lord in any flaming bush if they can't see him yonder?"

I saw the tree he meant, far up the hillside—a maple, glowing crimson against the dark pines.

" It's a wonderful place up there," he said, softly; "no one goes to it but me. That tree is high on a ledge of rock—very high; underneath it now the ground is all soft moss and violets—violets so thick you can't help but step on them. Later there's a single columbine, just at the edge of the rock—it stands out clear against the sky as you lie under the tree. You go up there very early—all below is mist, like a sea—a wonderful radiant sea, and the sun just touches the mountains beyond—then they become the Delectable Mountains. It's as if——-"

He stopped abruptly. " I beg your pardon," he said in his embarrassed, hesitating way, "I forgot. It's— it's so beautiful—and they don't see them—none of them!"

I looked at him for a moment in silence, and felt

as if I had always known him, just as I felt I had always known the little house and the apple trees—this strange shy fellow with his uncouthness and his fineness, his sudden vehemence.

"I came up here," I said slowly, "because I wanted to see the trees come alive. I think I must have heard them calling. Will you take me up the hill some day?"

"Yes," he said.

He looked off again to the hillside, pulled the old felt hat from his head. "If ever the time comes when I see no wonder nor liveliness in the springtime, but only the deadening round of monotonous work—may the Lord blind my eyes and stop my ears!"

That evening, after I saw McLeod pass down the hill, through the gate, I sat for a long time by the new garden picking up absently clod after clod of the soft earth he had ploughed, and crumbling them in my fingers, I looked off toward Stephen McLeod's Delectable Mountains. A thrush deep in the ravine uttered his note, another answered; then, far down the hill in the woods into which McLeod had disappeared,

another, faint in the distance, but very clear; then an answer to that.

"He's right," I said; "the wonder and the loveliness is the chief thing. I've been blind and deaf all my life!"

Chapter Twelve

For some reason Clark's garden did better than mine. I mean her garden bed with the retaining wall and the muck from the ravine for soil. The young wild things in it looked cheerful and sprightly; the ferns she had brought up the hill in the little cart grew as luxuriantly as if transplanting had never happened—they didn't turn a hair; the pansies I had set there throve lustily and began to blossom in lovely colors—they and the maindenhair ferns got on together charmingly. And yet apparently the only thing Clarky did for the bed was to give it pail after pail of water.

Mine was different; the little plants came up joyfully enough; the poppies changed from a soft green fuzz to real seedlings; the cornflowers were two or three inches high and had long, narrow gray-green leaves with a silver tinge.

Suddenly one after another of them flopped—toppled over as if unexpectedly faint. They didn't crumple in a heap as I did when I felt tired; but fell full length, like an eighteenth century novel-heroine. I had no idea what ailed them. I sat on my cushion by the flower-bed and stared at them in dismay; then I lifted one poor little cornflower carefully and tried to help it up, thinking it had simply fainted; but it was no use; it couldn't stand.

Just then Mrs. Tarbox came out; she had a couple of dish towels in her hand which she hung irreverently on the fragrant lilac that was coming into magnificent bloom.

"What's the matter?" she asked. "You look kinder peaked, Caroline."

"What's the matter with them?" I said, almost tearfully.

She bent laboriously, poked the poor limp things casually with a fat forefinger, then righted herself again. "Cutworms," she said—"cutworms; bit the stems off."

"But what can you do for them?"

"Cuss," responded Mrs. Tarbox briefly. "That's what folks does mostly."

"Isn't there anything else you can do?" I said in despair.

"Oh, yes, they's plenty of things you might do. But you don't notice the pesky things till they've up an' done it—bit the stems off—jus' like that. Then you get out your pizen bait an' what-not an' mos' wear yourself out fixin' it so's the worms'll get it an' the chickens won't; an' by the time you get it fixed, the evenin' an' the morning's the second day or the third day. Cutworms has had another bite—seedlings is all gone! If you're a swearin' man, you cuss; if you're a member of the Church an' a Christian woman, you set jus' like your're settin' now—an' think.

"Isn't there any way of getting ahead of them?" I asked blankly.

"They's ways enough," she said dispassionately, "but you ain't ahead. You're behind 'em Caroline."

"Is there nothing I can do?"

"Wa-al," she said, judicially, "next year, when you're plantin' seeds jes before they come up—then's the time to out with your pizen bait an' what-not. Then the cutworms is there—a-layin' there, jes under the surface, with their mouths waterin', eyeing them young things an' waitin' for them to be big enough to eat. Then they'll take the pizen bait like 'twas Manna-in-the-Wilderness."

"That's all I know 'bout cutworms, Caroline. Course, if you want, you can set up all night with a lantern, waitin' till they come out, an' when you see one, lamm him. You can make traps—poke holes, you know—hopin' they'll drop into them an' let you kill 'em in the mornin'. Maybe they will, an' maybe they won't. I've noticed they was pretty deft at steppin' round them."

"But if I was you, an' didn't know no more about plantin' than you seem to know, I'd jes' sow some fresh seed over to that new patch that Steve dug ('tain't likely they's worms there) an' when those get grown up big

enough, why, I'd move 'em into the front bed. Cause by that time the cutworms'll have got through an they'll let the things alone."

"Course, if you was more intelligent, more responsible-like, I'd give you different advice. But bein' who you are, I think that's the best you can do."

Whereat she left me and went into the house.

For a long time I sat there, looking blankly at the poor little cornflowers. Slowly, insistingly, it was borne in upon me that Mrs. Tarbox was right. Another person might do differently, I couldn't; I had neither courage, nor energy, nor intelligence to fight those horrible worms.

Moreover, Reason—the Reason that loomed large in Doctor Johnson's ideas, the Reason that poor Mary Wollstonecraft urged women to cultivate instead of Feeling—rose up and backed Mrs. Tarbox. It told me I hadn't prepared that garden-bed properly; that the grocer's boy had forked it, as it were, with a dessert fork; that it lacked depth, like the female intellect; that the only way to have a really good garden-bed in that place was to take out all the worthless soil, cutworms and all, and put in better.

Suddenly, all that in garden books I had passed over hastily to reach the more interesting parts, flashed accusingly before my mind like the handwriting on the wall before the dismayed Belshazzar. Phrase after phrase I recalled—"dig to the depth of two feet," "remove and replace with good garden soil," "should have deep, rich soil," "light, rich, sandy loam"—they became charged with meaning, freighted with significance. I felt like a young mother who, in a careless girlhood, has passed over as irrelevant , information on infants' diet, and for whom, her child sick and no doctor at hand, the aspect changes suddenly; that which was uninteresting and irrelevant has become vital, imperative, something it is almost criminal not to have known!

But these poor little things were done for! I make no defense of my conduct in thus abandoning the luckless seedlings to their fate; I simply admit that I did it. Napoleon abandoned his wounded in the Egyptian campaign; but I didn't feel like Napoleon.

Sadly, tenderly, I dug up the little survivors. I looked carefully at each root, then I set them in a pan of soapy water and carried them to the new garden, planted them there as skillfully as I knew how. And I humbly took Mrs. Tarbox's further advice, went into the house, got some fresh seed–packets and sowed in the new garden two rows of seed.

This done, I went indoors, curled up on the window-seat and read what I might have done about cutworms, very much as Red Riding-Hood's mother might have taken a natural history and read about the predatory habits of the wolf after he had swallowed her little daughter.

For the sad part was, I might have informed myself. Richard Protheroe, who had sent the Trimardeau pansies, had sagely followed his gift with one after another of his garden books—they had come at the rate of one a week. I suppose he hoped thereby to insure the safety of his beloved plants. But I had read none of them. The out-of-doors and the getting well had been too wildly interesting, the planting too exciting.

Of course I had poked in them a bit. One can't help poking in any new book. But that was all.

You see, garden books are of two kinds. There are rhapsodic ones which are excellent company when you're shut up in your room; then it's pleasant enough to see with the eyes of another. But when all the spring loveliness is yours just for opening your eyes and ears and taking in the breath of life in your nostrils, you aren't interested in the least in other people's rhapsodies, however impassioned—you can do it yourself; besides, there are the thrushes who express it very perfectly. It's like being made to read a translation of a poem when you can have the original.

As for the other sort—the hard-headed, practical books—they had seemed to me horribly prosaic; weariful, colorless, school-book prose, a mantle of Gradgrind fact that one's imagination lent to the planting of seed and flower, which for me had been full of charm and wild excitement.

It was the catalogues that had been my joy. The catalogues where, soberly arranged by Jane or Elizabeth or Mary Ann in their admirable gardens, but an account of the radiant beauty that was to spring from the very seed that I had dropped in the ground and which would arise—the wonderful creature—in all it's loveliness right outside my living-room window. That was the hope; and the hope had been devoured by cutworms.

Gardening is much like marriage. The catalogues are it's romantic novelists; they tell you little about the hazards and vicissitudes of the adventure, but dwell only on the "happy forever after" idea; the joy in the possession of the adored object. You don't think about cutworms when you plan a garden any more than people about to be married think of children with measles, and rent, and fleeting cooks—it's afterward.

Chapter Thirteen

The new garden was more hopeful. Stephen McLeod, for all his shiftlessness, had done the work well. Even Mrs. Tarbox said that.

First he ploughed it, as I said. He made long furrows curl over evenly until the "green-tressed goddess" became brown-tresssed, and looked as if she had been Marcelled; then he took the harrow, destroyed the Marcel effect, and gave our worthy Mother a more decorous coiffure—smooth and only slightly crimpy. Moreover, he brought manure and harrowed it in (which doesn't fit the simile unless you consider it hairdressing).

"He ain't so foolish about doin' the work," conceded Mrs. Tarbox, as she stood inspecting the smooth, brown square of the new garden, one evening just after Stephen had gone. "It's his way of goin' at it that's so crazy. Look how he's doin' here. 'Stead of givin' you two or three whole days' work, like any sensible man'd have done, here he is, stoppin' in and workin' an hour or two in the evenin' when he'd oughter be settin' down to home with his work all done. I ain't saying' it's hard on the horses—Steve's really foolish about horses, an' they don't hev far to go up the hill, but it—it ain't right!" she ended severely.

I liked Stephen's shameless way of doing things; it suited me exactly. We had our early supper (for Clarky and I kept children's hours), then she would spread a rug for me on the grass, as near as was safe to the scene of action—below the stone wall, where the roses lost themselves in the grass—and from there I watched the work.

It's the time of all others to be out-of-doors—the time that well-regulated folk devote to dinner. The daylight is clear as yet, but the hush of evening is unmistakable. Instead of their wonderful vespers, the thrushes, over in the deep woods, are uttering low, intimate notes—speech rather than song; for in this hush of the early evening, when quietness has fallen like a spell on all the out-of-doors, it is as if the marvelous new springtime, with all it's wonder and beauty and myriad life, were being put to sleep like a baby on the breast of it's Mother Earth.

I used to lie on the rug and watch the work—I could have watched for hours. I liked the motion of the man and the horses outlined against the sky.

As for Stephen, he worked in silence most of the time, but sometimes he would talk in his rapt, eager way. I liked that, but I never could tell what would start it.

"Why must you do that?" I asked him once. He had been standing over by the young poplars, lifting forkfuls of manure from a brown, velvety-looking pile, and with one fling scattering it over the ploughed ground with a motion as sure and graceful as if he had been throwing the discus. "Why does my garden need it? Those young poplars haven't extra rations, and they're thrifty enough."

"You're an invader," he said. "They're in their own country. Invaders always have the odds against them when they're driving out the rightful inhabitants of the land."

"They're the invaders," I said, looking at the lusty young poplars that had marched un-bidden into my land.

He shook his head. "It's fighting. It seems peaceful enough—the gardening and farming—but there's a bitter warfare under it all that never stops for a moment. That's why the farmers hate the wilderness so; there's been a sword between them for generations. They can drive the wild nature back and hold it at bay, but never has she ceded the land. Always she is watching; she throws back at them pests that never trouble her own. They have taken her kingdom by violence; if they relax their grasp for a moment, she seizes it and makes it her own again.

"Look over there!" he said, pointing across the wide acres, "a few years ago all this was farm. The road I go up was worn and traveled; it has violets in it now; all that," and he pointed past the barns, toward the fringing pines, "was mowing land, below the barns were field crops, corn and oats. And now, see! Do you see those little sharp brown spear-heads, hundreds and hundreds of them, down the slope and up the slope? Those are spireas, come in from the pasture. Look up the hill. See the sprinkling of dark green in the mowing? Those are seedling pines, come down from the pines on the hill. And here, you see, the woods are coming in. First the poplars, next will come oaks and beeches and maples, not so easy to dislodge. The wilderness is taking her own again!"

He laughed whimsically. "Can't you see how she does it? The haste and the gladness, as if it were a lost and beloved child come back to her. How she tries to make it forget the years of its captivity, covering with grass and violets the scars where the roads have bound it, bringing in trees and flowers and shrubs—whatever will grow the soonest, just as a robe was brought for the Prodigal, new shoes for his feet, and a ring for his hand, before he had entered the house!"

I looked about with a sudden, new interest. It was as he said. The wilderness was closing in, swiftly, inexorably, as the tide. Then I looked at the house serenely content in the late sunshine. "The little house doesn't mind." I said suddenly.

He looked at it, laughed again. "The little house doesn't mind," He repeated; then he glanced at the barns, standing gaunt and aloof. "Don't know about the barns," he added, casually, as he turned to his work. "Guess the barns are like Mrs. Tarbox; they think it ain't right!"

Chapter Fourteen

I was beginning to observe that the part of gardening that interested Clarky was what she would have called the "major operations." She liked pruning-shears very much as she liked a hammer; she liked retaining walls; she had climbed the apple tree and sawed off a dead limb, and I knew from the absorbed way in which she was looking at the catalogues that she was considering buying one of the interesting knapsack arrangements and spraying.

When the box of plants came—she had sent for it to a northern nursery because the planting season was late—she showed me how to cut the shrubs "hard

back" as she called it, for the leaves were starting, and "quiescence must be induced if they were to recover from the transplanting operation performed at an unfavorable time." She showed me how to clip from the inside and leave outside the "eye." But beyond this concern for the well-being of the plants, and telling me I must sprinkle them, put back the packing, and wait for Stephen to dig the holes, she offered no suggestions whatever about planting, until I wondered if she had been reading Doctor Montessori, or if she held Mrs. Tarbox's views, that my ignorance was so deep it was hardly worth enlightening.

No more did Stephen.

As soon as we began planting, he grew taciturn and relapsed into his old shyness.

The planting itself was interesting. The hollyhocks had roots like long, attenuated parsnips; the root of the iris was curious, it looked like a giant centipede—a thick bulbous thing with small rootlets dangling from it like innumerable legs. I hoped it would terrify the cutworms. I thought it might.

But Stephen's attitude bothered me; I had so liked it when he dropped the shyness and showed the pagan that he was that the change was disturbing. He set out plant after plant where I asked him to, but he would only answer me in monosyllables. I tried to "draw him out." I started subject after subject, but it was no use; they dropped as limply as the cornflowers when the cutworms were at their stems; he planted Frau Karl Druschki and Ulrich Brunner with the apathy of a farmer's boy doing reluctant chores. He was changed as completely from the fine pagan of whom I'd caught a glimpse as Browning's gypsy, who, after bewitching the little Duchess, drew her cloak about her and sank back into the mumbling crone.

I felt as disappointed as the little Duchess must have felt.

Then an idea struck me.

"You don't like my garden!" I said.

He shot me a quick, startled glance, very like the look the brown rabbit gave me in the mornings when, for an infinite second, it eyed me and considered whether to risk staying or to vanish.

"Don't know as I've said I didn't like your garden," he answered slowly, hesitatingly, bending again to firm the soil about Ulrich Brunner.

"But you don't!"

Again the quick, startled look. Then he stopped his work and straightened his shoulders. "No, I don't like your garden," he answered, simply.

"But why?"

"You're going to spoil things," he said, turning on me the blue gaze that had grown suddenly intense—"I thought it was going to be different, but it isn't. You're going to 'slick up' like all the rest of them! And this is the only unspoiled place in all Enderby!

"You have your ideas, your notions of what's—pretty," he explained calmly—"something you've seen or read about. And a different sort of beauty—a completer beauty—you don't see, just because it is different; you don't understand it; naturally you don't respect it."

I had my wish about Stephen's shyness. It was gone completely, he stood erect and was as serenely unembarrassed as one of the young poplars. I was the one who felt awkward and ill at ease, an alien and an intruder on the ground where he and they felt so sure of themselves.

For a few minutes I said nothing. Somehow there seemed to be nothing to say. Then I, in turn, looked at him nervously, wondering which were worse, whether he would think me more foolish if he really knew how I had gone a-gardening, or if he kept his present view and thought my sins deliberate. "He can't think worse," I concluded.

"Mr. McLeod," I said at last, "I am more ignorant than you think, but I love this little place; if I'm spoiling it, it's just a blunder, not intentional. And as for my gardening——"I hesitated a moment; then I told him about Uncle Hermann and his roses, and how I wanted to touch the roses with my fingers and to train them myself; how I wanted to have my fingers in the soil, to plant the seeds myself and watch them grow, how I wanted to see the trees come alive that Clarky had talked about, "and as for this rather motley array of plants," I said, deprecatingly, "I choose them because I knew them; or liked their names; I did have planting plans when I was ill, but the only plan I have now is to get them into the ground as fast as possible, for Clarky says it's late."

To my surprise, Stephen looked positively relieved. "And you aren't ` improving' the place?" he said.

I shook my head. "Tell me what I'm doing that's wrong! I love it here; I'd like to treat the genii loci as well as did Mabel on Midsummer Day. But you know them better than I. How am I going to spoil things? What is wrong? How would you plant?"

"I wonder if you would see," he said slowly. "People think I am daft, but, Lordy, how much they miss! And what months and years of labor and what oceans of money to wipe out one kind of beauty and replace it by another that doesn't fit but is something that can have 'I did it' written on it."

"This little place has done that rare thing— made friends with the wild. And it's easy to spoil a friendship!"

"But how am I going to spoil it?"

"It is not one great thing that can spoil the charm—it's the small things, so slight you think them unimportant. Those roses for one," He answered, looking at Ulrich Brunner. If you grow them properly, cut down to two or three stems, buds pinched off and that sort of thing, you'll have some fine blooms, but you will make those old cinnamons feel out of place—and they are beautiful as they are. Your lilacs will never be at home with the poplars—I'd put them by the kitchen door and the woodshed."

"Mme. Casimir-Perier?" I asked.

"Certainly," he said indifferently—"lilacs are homely things—like to be near habitations. I'd put the Japanese iris over there in the damp hollow, yonder where the cat-tails are common."

"But I won't see them!"

"You can go and look at them," said he carelessly.

"But they are rare varieties and the cat-tails are common."

Stephen looked at me curiously.

"It's the gardener's flowers that are common," he said. "No wild rose was ever as common—even vulgar—as a crimson rambler is sometimes; but it's coarsened. Beauty of form, grace, delicacy, perfectness of poise, exquisite fitness of the flower to its surroundings—these are sculptor's values—but they're values and it is in the wild that you find them. Put a heavily scented, heavy-headed violet that has lost all its shapeliness beside a white wood violet as you find it—invariably exquisitely placed—and to me it looks like one of those horrible, overfed restaurant women that you see in New York, beside a wood nymph."

"Sculptor's values!" I said to myself.

Then I, in turn, looked at Stephen curiously.

"If you live with the wild long enough," he said, "you'll feel like Saint Peter after he saw the vision, that in it there is nothing common—unless we twist and change and make it so."

So it happened, that after all my planning, I did my garden more or less after the "gospel according to Stephen" as Clarky would say, when I quoted him.

He showed me where, in the mowing, below the barn, were old red roses of my grandmother's garden, almost strangled by the grass, and we dug them up and brought them home. And I put Iris, the many-colored goddess, over in the damp hollow where the farthest woodchuck could survey it as he sat at his house door and I had to make a pilgrimage for the sight. And I planted the lilacs, even Mme. Casimir-Perier and Charles the Tenth, by the kitchen door and the woodshed corner. I put the flowering almond near the doorstep, and the hollyhocks next the window where my poor cornflowers and been.

"If the house were more elaborate," I explained to Clarky, who eyed the planting with some disfavor, "we would need an elaborate garden to connect it with the wild, but you see this little place has made perfect connections already."

"Is your friend McLeod a landscape gardener?" she inquired.

"The most difficult thing in art is to know when to let alone," I said. "I reckon Stephen knows that."

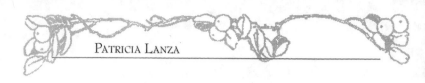

The garden proper grew more and more utilitarian, and in its laying out I took the advice of Mrs. Tarbox, who bestowed that commodity frankly, if unflatteringly.

"Plant them seeds in rows, Caroline," she advised "and don't try anything fancy till you know more. An' when you know more," she added sagely, "you won't try it. If they ain't in rows, you'll be pullin' up your posies 'cause you can't tell 'em from the weeds. But if you see a straight row comin' up—all one kind of leaf—you'll sense that. It may be Scripture for the tares an' the wheat to grow together, but if I do say it as shouldn't, the wheat'll grow lots better if the tares was yanked out. An' you want to be so's you can yank 'em out."

Again I considered Mrs. Tarbox's advice. Again I followed it.

All sorts of annuals I planted—poppies, mignonette, godetia, gaillardia, and the rest; and all sorts of vegetables. The vegetables and the flowers alternated cheerfully. I edged beds of marigolds and of poppies with lettuce; and I bordered rows of vegetables with dwarf marigolds and nasturtium and mignonette. Feebly, in

the rush of belated planting, I tried to follow my plan and at least arrange the colors for peace and comfort.

"Land sakes!" said Mrs. Tarbox, "you'll be doin' well if they grow up an' flower at all, an' if you have any eatin' out of the garden-stuff 'thout fussin' 'bout effects. You can't tend to too many thins to once, Caroline! If you keep a-fussin' 'bout color effects, first thing you know some pest or other has et up your plants and they ain't any effect al all, 'ceptin' the one your disposition of disappointment. Just you try an' see if you can keep the weeds out, an' keep the bugs off, an' remember that handsome is as handsome does!"

Chapter Fifteen

The middle of June Mrs. Tarbox left us. She said I was now and 'round; that her housecleaning had been let go so long that if "Twan't done next week she didn't know what she would do!"

Alonzo had come to fetch her. Thad had just driven down the hill, leaving Clarky and me sitting on our doorstep in the dusk of the Sunday evening, considering the situation.

Clarky spoke of one and another whom Mrs. Tarbox had said "might help us out."

"They's Mis' Rayford," Mrs. Tarbox had said, "but you'll have to fetch her an' take her home. An' they's

Josie Pratt to the foot of the hill; she might come an' wash up for you."

The thrushes were singing adorably, just as they always did at dusk—fluting out arpeggios that went dizzily, divinely, high. It seemed wicked to be considering the question of whether Josie Pratt would wash our dishes or whether she wouldn't to such an ecstatic accompaniment—as bad as Mrs. Tarbox's dish towels on the lilac bush.

"Anything we imported," said Clarky, surveying our wide dooryard that reached acres and acres across to the fringing pines, "wouldn't stay—too lonesome."

There was a long silence, broken only by the sound of the church-bells that reached us faintly from the little church across the river.

"Clarky," I said at last, "every wild creature over in those woods has wit enough to get food for itself without being served by another. That thrush has found breakfast and luncheon and dinner and yet has leisure for his wonderful music. Why cannot you and I be clever enough to devise some form of rations that

will give us enough to eat and not consume our whole time, in this lovely June weather, in it's cooking and preparation."

Clarky turned and looked at me attentively for a moment, but she said nothing. She continued watching a chipmunk that sat on our new stone wall (searching for fleas I regret to say).

"The loveliest thing we have up here," I continued, "is our solitude. Why must we spoil it? Why glue our lives to a three-meal-a-day orbit with the kitchen stove as its governing sun? Why drape our lilac bushes with dish towels? The life is more than meat and the body more than raiment. We've simplified the raiment; why cannot we arrange the matter of meat?"

"Listen," I proceeded, "you can see to it that we have a properly balanced ration—carbohydrates, proteins, and all that—Heaven knows I don't want to be ill again—but for the rest, we can have bread and butter and eggs and cheese sent from the store, we can import zwieback and hard-tack. We can live on rice like the Japanese or on baked potatoes like Robert Browning.

And on a rainy day we can have a very orgy of cooking, if you like."

"Beside, I'm not so limp as I once was. I could do some 'chores.' There's no work so noble for a woman as domestic housework," I said, warming to the subject, Nothing that so suitably exercises body and soul and spirit as the care of a house and the preparation of food; nothing in which it is so essential that a woman train her daughter, so that—"

"So that if she doesn't marry," broke in Clarky, "she is sure of a situation in which there is little competition. I know all that sort of thing. You've read that in the women's magazines that are edited by men and in articles written by women who don't do it. I've seen plenty of women broken down by housework, and farmers' wives go insane from the monotony of this same charming occupation."

"It's the monotony, not the work," I protested. "There's no need of its being monotonous."

Then I expounded my theory. That if we lived out-of-doors, the house would keep in good order;

that with grass to the doorstep and no furniture, how could there be dusting? We could breakfast on wild strawberries—not spend an hour or so picking them, but go up the hill and bring ourselves to the breakfast. For our supper we could go to the doorstep with bread and milk, like Wordsworth's Little Cottage Girl, and we could "take our little porringers and eat our supper there." I explained to her that we would consider the season; we would put the unavoidable "chores" into that part of the day which out-of-doors was the least interesting. As for the dishes, once a day they could be piled in the little cart and I could trundle them to the brook. I would place them carefully in the gravel, then, while I was taking my nap, the brook would be kind enough to wash them. Undoubtedly they would be quite as well done as by Jose Pratt, and how infinitely more poetic the operation! Thus we would save the most valuable part of the day for the June Weather."

"According to the thrushes," I said, " the evening and the morning are the time for spiritual refreshment.

The woodchucks seem to be at liberty at three in the afternoon."

Clarky looked at me keenly. "Sounds like Mr. Stephen McLeod." She remarked.

"I hope it does," I answered. "Mr. McLeod is a man of much intelligence and a fine sense of proportion."

Clarky took off her spectacles, pushed her dark hair back as she always did when considering deeply.

"Miss Caroline," she said, at last, "there are always chores, plain, unaffected, unattractive, unavoidable chores, even in keeping a place like this in order. No amount of garlanding with poetry, or of obscuring with Stephen McLeod's hallucinations will make them less chores. Some days it will be amusing to "tote the dishes to the brook," as you say. Some days it won't. And on the days when it isn't amusing, the thing has still to be done. That is the very devil of housework— its incessant recurrence."

"However, make a good laundry connection; get a fireless cooker; have Mrs. Tarbox or her equivalent once a week, and I'm with you. The wild-strawberry breakfast

is no good; grass is too wet; as for the Little Cottage Girl supper—she took her bread and milk to the cemetery, if I remember correctly, where were the little brother and sister who probably died of improper diet or imperfect sanitation; but the rest is possible. But—-

"But what?" I asked.

"It strikes me you're getting well," she said.

Chapter Sixteen

It was after Mrs. Tarbox's departure that Aunt Cassandra began to get a bit nervous about me.

She needn't have been; we were absurdly happy. For the first time in my life the days were one long picnic—that's not the right word, for a picnic can be deadly boring. Rather, shall I say, that the days were full of joyous adventure, and as for any sense of Duty, I think I must have planted it at the bottom of the very deep, post-like hole we dug for the deep-rooted hollyhock. Even the cutworms ceased from troubling; and as for the garden, Glarky had a charming little cultivator, a

very arsenal in the completeness of its equipment. It was plough and cultivator and marker, a sod cutter and sower and weeder—everything combined. Moreover, it was good to look upon; its handles were painted red, its teeth and action parts a fine grass green. Clarky took the greatest delight in trying its various stops and gaits and grears. With all its complexity of resource, the little thing was light to handle, and once a week she pushed it between the rows. That was the weeding!

As for the watering—she got an interminable length of rubber hose, fastened it on our one faucet in the kitchen, led it out the window, and down the garden or around the house. Then she'd turn on the faucet in the kitchen and let the water run between the furrows as if she were irrigating; the day after, she cultivated; then, for a week, we let the garden alone. And the plants flourished; they grew like the wicked and the green bay tree.

"The simple life," said Clarky, as she stood surveying her irrigation scheme, "is only possible when labor is reduced to a minimum by up-to-date conveniences."

Also once a week did Stephen come up. That was Sunday afternoon. He had stock, he said, in the pasture above us, and had to go up the hill "to see if everything was all right."

But Aunt Cassandra, as I said, was worried. She thought we lived on the unsatisfactory and insufficient diet to which the babes in the woods were reduced. But she was wrong! Our commissariat department went on charmingly. We kept one eye on nutrition, the other on possible dishes. We breakfasted on fruit and prepared cereal, and boiled eggs in a chafing dish on the table and ate them from the shells. After breakfast, the milk and butter went down cellar, while the dishes were shamelessly piled in a pan and covered with water. Clarky would wash the silver—I couldn't corrupt her utterly—but the hot water in the chafing dish sufficed for the few knives and spoons, and , as she said, "the operation was simple, almost painless."

After breakfast we addressed ourselves to the out-of-doors. We had a variety of enterprises on hand. Clarky was jacking up the woodshed by a cleverly arranged

system of levers, ending in a long piece of scantling whereon she would have me sit while she thrust a block in precisely the right spot. This was highly interesting, and under her treatment, the woodshed, which had threatened to divorce itself completely from the house, bade fair to return to an amicable separation, perhaps in time to complete union.

Clarky also was making a lattice for the roses to climb upon when they were ready to do so; and she had some cans of ready-mixed paint which were the joy of her heart and an unfailing solace on a wet day. She painted the pink-and-drab woodwork that distressed our eyes and made it a dull green; she "sized" the kitchen walls with some stuff that smelt abominably in the process, and then painted them. She said it was extraordinary that people could deliver over these joys to a housepainter and be content to forfeit the feeling of proud achievement.

For myself, I worked quite steadily at the thinning and transplanting. Thinning is a heartrending occupation; you can't help feeling sorry for the little plants to which you refuse a chance of life. Clarky said it was garden eugenics and scolded me for sentimentality, but I so hated throwing away the sorts that won't transplant that I used to try transplanting them, and I found I could move even poppies if I went about it properly, taking them when the ground was rather damp and, instead of digging up individual plants, taking a chunk of earth and all that grew thereon. I moved morning glories from one place where they swarmed and put them where they could climb against the house. I moved cornflowers and marigolds into the bed that the cutworms had devastated, dug up plants of sweet alyssum and made an edge of them. Then I watered, thoroughly soaking until they must have been wet to the tips of the roots, and sheltered them with an elaborate arrangement of shutters taken off the house.

I worked quite creditable every morning, and the little chipmunk used to sit on the wall and watch as if he hadn't an earthly thing to do. The fox sparrows didn't watch nor the thrushes, they were too busy. The fox sparrows were building in the big lilac bush, but they would only pause for a second, to see if I were a safe person, or to snatch a bit of packing-moss for their nest. A pair of adorable bluebirds had taken a hole in my apple tree for their residence. "My apple tree," did I say? "It's our apple tree," they told me plainly every time I went near it. And the woodpecker, who inspected it every morning as carefully as if he were an assiduous landlord, assured both the tenants and myself that it was his apple tree. I think he not only drilled for the housebreaking worms and borers but listened, as if he could hear them moving under the bark. What ears!

It was a busy, energetic, purposeful life upon which I had "intruded," in Stephen McLeod's words. Before I was well awake in the mornings I could hear the bees humming in the apple blossoms, and back and forth they went all day, tirelessly. There was fighting, love-making, quarrelling, but no ennui; apparently there was no time for gossip nor for watching one another's affairs. Each was keenly intent on his own business. Truly, I would have felt ashamed had I not been at work. Never did an East Side parent labor harder to feed the little mouths than did the swallows later in the summer; back and forth from the barn flew the fathers and mothers incessantly, and always the open mouths awaiting them, none shut but for an instant. I thought it would have discouraged the parents; but it didn't, for the next summer there would be another brood.

There's nothing whatever in the idea the poets give one sometimes, of birds sauntering about the sky, floating on idle pinions. They are quite as industrious as Dr. Watt's bees, only they make no noise about their work and are the gladdest things in existence.

Chapter Seventeen

In spite of the admirable example set by our tenants, we weren't always industrious. Sometimes we would put our dinner (in a more or less embryonic state) into the little cart and go for the day into the pasture across the ravine. We would take potatoes to roast, bacon to broil over the coals, hoe cakes to bake in the ashes.

It was a wonderful pasture, that of mine. Although they seemed so very deep—those woods where the thrushes lived—it was but a narrow strip of forest reaching down from the pines on the hill to shelter the little brook and see it safely to the river. Across the ravine and beyond them, lay the pasture. On my side, the landscape was beautiful, but quiet and gentle and wonderfully friendly; a place of softly modulated slopes, of lovely lines melting one into another, a tender and intimate beauty. Here in the pasture, everything was different. It was rough and strong and massive; great rocks pushed their shoulders through the thin pasture sod like uneasy giants, restless in their sleep, impatient of a covering grown cumbersome; the great bulk of the hill rose bare and uncompromising, its magnificent lines unsoftened by foliage, as if the very bone and sinew of the old earth were exposed. Of the forest with which it had once been clad, only three or four great pines were left like vanquished Titans that by a miracle had escaped the destruction that had overtaken their fellows. These stood, huddled together, powerless for all their vast strength, raising huge, shattered branches to the sky. And, like a lovely picture, framed by the giant pines on one side and the great oaks and beeches of the ravine on the other, very far below, lay the river and the quiet meadows, curiously peaceful and detached.

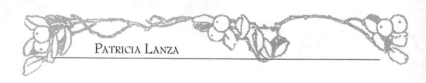
We went so often that we knew it all intimately. We knew each individual Jack-in-the-pulpit that we passed in going down the steep little path to the brook; we watched them, week by week, grow in size and importance as their audience increased; we knew the Solomon's seal that leaned its slender stem over the brook that its tiny bells might look at themselves in the water; the wild ginger that lived close to the water, stooping its red-brown cup as if to drink from the rushing little brook; we stepped carefully aside for a tiny white wood violet—a darling little sprite of a plant that grew directly in our path, settled comfortably in the crook of a tree-root, set on a cushion of bright green moss with a baby hemlock no taller that itself for company.

And the color! Here might the cunningest couturier come for hints. How was it that the fungus on the fallen brown oaks took such marvelous tones of orange, and that on the beeches varied through every shade of gray to rose and crimson? Past the brook, the woods were level and open, a fairy-book forest with wide aisles into which the sun came faintly. There were great beeches and oaks, and one cleft and hollow beech were Ariel might have been pent—and been fairly comfortable. Under foot the carpet of brown, dead leaves was gay with checkerberries and ground pine and in it grew lovely wild things—fringed polygala and foam flower, fragile star flowers, each borne on the slenderest of thread-like stems above the circlet of pointed leaves.

Evidently Madame Nature has the poorest opinion of her human children. Let them establish them selves, and she hastens to withdraw her darlings to safety, hurries away the most delicate of her dainty wild things, and throws back plantain and burdocks and witch grass, as destructive children are given playthings that they can't hurt; and at the same time, she scatters her loveliness over the bleak and unvisited pastures for the cows to tread on and the woodchucks to browse over, supremely careless as to whether it's seen or no by human folk.

In the pasture she was royally spendthrift. She clad her old sleeping giant of a hill with a mantle wonderfully embroidered in changing colors. Green was the groundwork—the thin light green of the pasture sod, the bordering trees for fringes. Then began the decoration; first, the faint showing of anemones at the edges; then thoughout the green showed the purple and gold of cinquefoil and blue violet; then bluets, misting over the green with their exquisite color, the faint young blue of the April sky. When the bluets grew fewer and fainter, she starred it over with wild strawberry blossoms, like tiny white wild roses, and swaying above them, as lightly poised as a dragonfly over a pool, the columbine. Then she changed the scheme for daises in white and gold and, underfoot, deep blue heal-all and the tiny bright red strawberries; so on through the summer and autumn, change after change, with never a pause and never a break, shifting imperceptibly from the dull rose of spirea to the gorgeous yellow of goldenrod, as a skilled musician changes the key and keeps the harmony.

I never tired of watching things in the pasture, of poking into the mounds of moss for the fairy cups and elf-needles. Clarky used to bring a book with her, but I'd as soon thought of bringing a book to the opera. Usually we camped near the woods, at the edge of the pasture where were marvelous mounds of moss— not the close velvet that creeps over the rocks, making gorgeous skullcaps for the old graybeards. This was deep and soft, and in structure like a miraculously tiny forest in which the checkerberries glowed like huge crimson lanterns; here were all the flowers of the pasture in very rare editions, violets tall and slender and wonderful in color; and bluets, not so close set as in the open, but delicate and solitary, like the star flowers, and beside them tiny hemlocks and beech trees not any taller than a violet, and hovering above them, columbines. I could have watched it contentedly the whole day. Clarky, when she tired of reading, used to cut a thin sapling of black birch, and make, with her jack-knife, odd little bread-and-butter knives for our use.

Then, when the sun grew low, we would go home again to the childish supper at the doorstep with the thrushes and the friendly chipmunks for company.

Truly a quiet life, but a happy one, and I was still weak enough to have excuse for this idleness.

Chapter Eighteen

At the end of June Aunt Cassandra's anxiety took a more tangible form.

"Our friend Richard," she wrote, "spends the Sabbath at Tavistock, which is, I believe, but a short distance beyond you. He has kindly offered to tarry a day at Enderby and ascertain something of your way of life, and the character of your occupations, which seem to me extraordinary and unsuitable."

"What a nuisance!", said I, irreverently.

Clarky looked up from her letters—she had brought the mail up from the foot of the hill and sat beside me on the doorstep reading a letter of her own, the mail bag at her feet. "Why?" she asked, "What's wrong?"

I read aloud from Aunt Cassandra—

"Well," she repeated, "What's wrong? What's he like? The pansies are a good sort, and good plants; the books are intelligent, neither drivel nor those near-fact things, pretty to look at and no earthly use if you want to plant. I've seen so many fool things sent to invalids I should think him rather intelligent. Isn't he? What is he like?"

"Thin, rather tall, smooth-shaven," I said meditatively, "he wears spectacles—the large round lenses that they make in Boston."

"That's nothing against him," said Clarky quickly.

"Dark hair," I continued, "and one lock always falls forward and hits the edge of his spectacles—it makes you nervous. He has a greenhouse and likes to potter in it— and a garden. But he's a young clergyman, Clarky, and he used to send me his sermons!"

"Weren't they good sermons?" she demanded.

"Oh, yes, well thought out—slightly socialistic—but

I didn't want problems. And poetry, Clarky! He would send that, too!"

"Good?" she inquired.

"Wearying. The form was after Rossetti; sometimes there would be a roughness and an apparent force that was Browningesque; you'd think something was coming surely; but the utterance, when it came, was—Tupper! It worried one's mind. Always I would think I was going to get something; always I wouldn't."

"But the poetry has stopped?" asked Clarky, as if making a diagnosis.

I nodded.

"Sermons and a greenhouse and spectacles and socialism—" she meditated.

"Oh, and a violin. He really plays well—very well."

"—And a violin," she amended, thoughtfully. There was a moment's silence.

"The Reverend Richard will like it up here," she said at last. "he'll want to stay."

Although the day was Wednesday, and it would be two days, Friday, at least, before Richard Protheroe descended on us, or to speak more literally, ascended to us—Clarky went indoors presently and began to prink the house. The same instinct, I suppose, that makes a woman pat her hair and look in the glass when a visitor is announced. She dusted, not that that was extraordinary occurrence, but rarely necessary— there was more dust in one morning in town than in three weeks on our hill. She cut long sprays of the cinnamon roses and put them in the stone crock on the window-sill. Then she began to polish the andirons.

This wasn't altogether vanity on behalf of the house, for if Richard was to report us to Aunt Cassandra, naturally we wanted him to carry back grapes of Eschol, as it were, rather than any report of giants in the land.

While Clarky was doing this I sat on the doorstep and looked at the flower-beds that ran alongside the house. Then I, too, rose up and followed her example; I began to prink the garden. I got the hose and washed the faces of the pansies and the maindenhair in Clarky's garden-bed, and a darling little bit of Herb Robert that was coming into bloom from a chink in the wall, until they looked as fresh and cheerful as a baby after a bath. Then I went around the corner to see the larger garden. Richard was something of an expert in a shy, quiet way, and I felt a little like a Sunday-school superintendent surveying his school, just before the children are to give a programe. There were all the bright little faces in nicely kept rows. To me, the garden looked very creditable.

The lettuce-border was a gay, fresh green, for whenever we wanted it for salad we pulled intervening plants so that the continuity of the border would be undisturbed; there was a row of stocky little marigolds, of prosperous looking cornflowers, of poppies that had spread into a soft mat of filmy gray-green foliage— buds there were, but they still held their heads down; on the coreopsis little, hard, dark red buttons were beginning to show. The roses hadn't done much; they were leafing out in a faint, ineffectual way. It must have been too late when I planted them. The zinnias and the marigolds had been my salvation. They could move with as much ease and alacrity as a New York family born and raised in apartments. Wherever was a gap, wherever something "had happened," wherever was barrenness or blankness from any cause, I would dig up a zinnia and it would fill the breach; or, if it didn't suit because of the color (my zinnias were all in shades of pink), then I would dig up a marigold and plant that there instead.

In spite of Mrs. Tarbox's mandate I did make the garden more comfortable as to color. Two hills of squash had been taken by the enemy; but the third, which seemed impregnable, was making a handsome mound. So I dug clumps of blue cornflowers and set them at the four corners, making the squash the centre, and it bid fair to look very decorative. Whenever a plant was worrying its neighbors, I dug it up and put it where it wouldn't. Of course, it's undeniably better to do this beforehand, and let each begin life in precisely the right place. But if one doesn't know enough for this, what else can one do?

So now I dug some more zinnias, tucked them into lonesome-looking places in the front garden, soaked the bed, and shaded it carefully.

The Reverend Richard appeared sooner than we thought.

It may have been due to the curve of the hill, or perhaps to the grassed-over state of the road, but, whatever the cause, never (unless they possessed a very creaky wagon) were we aware of the approach of visitors. They didn't approach—they appeared as suddenly as the angels appeared to Abraham as he sat at his tent door.

That very evening, as we (like Abraham) sat at our door consuming our simple meal, Richard appeared, framed between the smaller lilac bush and the apple tree. As suddenly as if a curtain had been raised, there he was—clericals, hat and stick, the lock of hair falling over on his spectales' rim, just as it did the last time I had seen him, three years before. The immaculate black of his trousers was dusty and his square-toed shoes also bore traces of the Enderby river road. Evidently he had walked up from the station. He pulled out an immaculate handkerchief and wiped his forehead.

"I am looking—" he began doubtfully; then he stopped abruptly. "My word, but you've gotten well!" he said, and he looked at me with sudden interest, and at Clarky with genuine admiration.

Clarky certainly had grown good to look upon these days. Her cheeks had tanned until they were the color of apricots; she wore a white blouse, as she always did, open at the throat, which showed the lovely line of neck and chin, and her hair was in two thick braids like an Indian squaw's. I liked to look at her myself, and I didn't wonder that Richard's eye lightened as he saw her framed in the doorway. Presently she vanished, to bring more refreshment (as Abraham did also, I believe, in the matter of the angels), and she reappeared in a moment later with a refilled pitcher and another bowl.

Richard fetched a bench from below the lilac bush, and we resumed our repast.

Richard beamed at the landscape; then he beamed at us; he said it was as lovely a spot as one would wish to find this side of Paradise. Then he told us the town news,

which somehow seemed a bit irrelevant, as we listened to the thrushes and consumed the childish supper.

"What does this make you think of, Richard?" I asked, after a pause.

"Pilgrim, refreshed at the house of Mercy?" he inquired.

"Farther back—six-year-old reading."

He looked at the house, at us, at the little table and the three bowls of varying sizes, then laughed a boy-like and unclerical chuckle. "The 'Three Bears'?" he said.

Clarky was right about Richard.

He liked it. He stayed until I began to fear he would break his neck or at least his spectacles in finding his way down the hill, for there was a blind turn you take, and an unwary step would send you crashing violently down a steep place like the wicked stepmother in the fairy-tale. I had to lend him our one little lantern. He was staying the night at Mrs. Tarbox's; he purposed prospecting on our hill for sites for apple and nut orchards. He would come tomorrow and "spy out the land," he said.

Chapter Nineteen

Richard, as I said, liked it. He stayed by the doorstep that first evening watching the sky and listening to the thrushes until they stopped singing and the dusk fell and the crickets began their steadily insistent "Go in! Go in! Go in!" which ought to have sent him down the hill to Mrs. Tarbox's. But it didn't.

Instead, he came indoors to our crackling wood fire which made the hemlock branches cast queer, flickering shadows on the walls, and flashed from his large lensed spectacles. He sat on the floor by the fire, regardless of his clericals, long arms clasped about his knees, and told us his plans, also the theories which were responsible for the plans.

I took the invalid's privilege of the window-seat and cushions, for I was tired. Clarky sat opposite Richard on the other side of the fireplace, her back toward me, but her back looked interested. She leaned forward, chin on her hand, and listened as if it were a medical lecture and she were taking notes.

Richard was terrible in earnest. He always was over his theories. He talked farming conditions to Clarky as if her soul's salvation depended upon his getting his idea "across to her", as the playwrights.

At last I woke up to what he was saying. "Here?" I broke in. "A pastorate up here?"

"Precisely," he answered, turning the gleaming spectacles upon me. "The most important problem in the country is the industrial problem; the only part of this I understand is where it touches agriculture. Therefore it behooves me to establish myself where the problem is agriculture. Nowhere is the agricultural problem in sorer need of intelligent solution than in New England."

"But the salary, Richard! There are plenty of anemic and paralytic churches. There's a brick one over the hill, really good architecture, and an old orchard beside, and the country may be good for fruit raising, but the salary! Four or five hundred a year—-something like that, Mrs. Tarbox told me—no one could possibly live on that!"

"But that's the interesting part, my dear Caroline," said Richard mildly, "I shall then have precisely the problem the farmers of the neighborhood face without the aid of that stipend. It will be enlightening to find if one is adequate."

Then he explained his theory. He said the idea of a clergyman insulated from the problems of the community, was un-socialistic, undemocratic, it was also un-apostolic; he held it a man's duty, especially nowadays, to lead his flock economically as well as spiritually into green pastures; that he should assist his people to live rather than live off them.

"Nowhere is better farming more necessary than in New England—for the lack of it the young folk go cityward and the farmer's kingdom is taken from him

by the summer resident, and the man from outside who knows how to farm better."

"It is well enough to have ancestors who came over in the Mayflower," said Richard, "and the distance from which we view them undoubtedly enhances their worth, but farming methods should be more recent. Surely three hundred years is sufficient time for people to discover that their climate conditions are not England's watery sky; that drought in the summer may be counted on almost as certainly as flowers in the spring, and that it would be well to make some provision for it aside from praying for rain. New England farming is archaic."

"There's plenty of modern machinery," said Clarky.

"Yes, but look at it, my dear Miss Clarke. Left out in the rain and dew—treatment which might have been accorded harmlessly to the wooden Egyptian plough of Moses's time, but which is deadly to iron and steel mechanism."

"The Pilgrim Father was a worthy soul," continued Mr. Protheroe, "but he robbed the land just as he robbed the Indian. "The Earth is the Lord's and the fullness thereof," was his idea, and, moreover, that the Lord had delivered it into his hand, wherefore he may take all and give nothing back. His descendant does precisely the same thing—wastes the fertilizer, wastes the resources of the land, wastes the digestion of his boys and girls, wastes the strength of his cattle. Father and son for two hundred and fifty years will be content to lose ten years from the life of every horse on the farm rather than to change a road and give an easy grade instead of one which puts a terrific strain on the animals.

"It is not economy the farmer has, my dear Miss Clarke, not economy, but congestion of the purse strings! No wonder he and Mother Nature clash, as you say your friend here tells you. His policy is one of devastation, of conquest, and the bare, scraped hills are witness to it."

"It is socialism that farming needs," said Richard, warming to his pet subject, "socialism and Montessori methods of education. Cooperation of the land is varied, the crops should suit the diverse abilities of the soil, a kind of vocational training should be followed.

Thus we have from Madame Nature cooperation and assistance rather than enimity." He quoted Saint Paul to the effect that on a farm all parts are "members one of another, but all members have not the same office." "Why force it on them?" he inquired.

"When trees are so gifted by Nature," said he, "that their roots can force their way through the rocks down to the cool, moist soil below—why should we painfully and laboriously remove the rock for them and teach the roots to come near the surface so that in summer watering becomes a necessity, although at that season the streams run dry?"

There was, in his mind, no reason why our bare hills might not be covered with prosperous apple and cherry and nut orchards, as the Italian hills are covered with the olive trees. His intention, it seemed, was to establish nut orchards and to get a small piece of land into a very high state of cultivation instead of having a large area indifferently productive.

He considered the whole problem of the hill country an agricultural problem. He bade us remember that the undoubtedly familiar story of the Exodus was the account of an exploited people leaving an exploited industry and betaking themselves to country life and farming, each on his own holding, in the Land of Canaan. Thus and much more, Mr. Protheroe.

I grew tired and listened rather absently, but Clarky sat enthralled. It fitted so admirable with her own ideas, which always makes any one's discourse more interesting.

Clarky held the unflattering belief that all bodily ills came from being more or less of a fool in the ordering of one's life, and omitting three square meals a day.

She told me afterward, as she was helping me to bed (for she still kept the nurse's habit in that respect), that it was perfectly simple; that what ailed the farms was, as she made out from Richard's discourse, a kind of nervous exhaustion—overwork, lack of nourishment, no diversion—always the same kind of work, and a possibly distasteful occupation at that. She understood it perfectly, and thought it very interesting.

"There's quite a bit in his theory," said she," and I

agree with him that the chief causes of rural decadence are the country minister and the country school. These teachers who should lead are followers, and followers a long way behind."

"You have a good memory for the Reverend Richard's remarks, Clarky," I said, "but there's nothing new in his theory."

"The willingness to try it out is new," said she.

"But how can he have time for study if he carries out all these lovely farming experiments?"

"Study!" said Clarky. "When you study defective physical and sanitary conditions you go where they are and experience them, or you go to a hospital and see the people who are ill from them. You experiment and prove, or your theory is no good. He is simply for trying out his social and religious theory. It's perfectly intelligent, perfectly scientific—a bully idea."

Chapter Twenty

Next morning, I was sitting on the doorstep having my early coffee—the one dissipation our hill afforded—when Richard appeared. It was not yet seven. Evidently the climate had something the same effect on the Reverend Richard that it had on Clarky. Instead of clericals he was all in khaki—very new—with canvas leggings—also new—and a soft hat something like Stephen's might once have been. In his hand was a Delft blue dinner-pail.

"Where's Miss Clarke?" said he.

He carefully set down the dinner-pail on the step,

that Mrs. Tarbox's pie, which I knew it contained, might not be jarred. Then he sat down beside me.

"Where's Miss Clarke?" he repeated.

"Off to the farm for extra milk." I said. "She won't be back for nearly three quarters of an hour. Have some of my coffee?"

Richard went inside and found a cup with more skill and expedition than I thought he had, and sat down beside me again. The mist still lay in the valley, although the top of the mountain was clear. Old Ascutney looked as if he had pulled the fleecy blanket up to his chin, and intended taking another nap.

"How long have you been doing this," asked he, "keeping these very sprightly hours?"

"Coffee on the doorstep? More than a month."

"You've been getting wonderfully well," said he, "How has it been accomplished?"

"Digging in the ground," I answered.

"Back to the soil very literally?"

I nodded, then set down my cup. "Yes, it's the garden," I said, slowly, "though I dare say you think it doesn't look like much, but I never did it myself before. There's something wonderfully soothing in having your fingers in Mother Earth. It seems to take the restlessness out of one. Then, you know, when I've tried to get well before, the only way was to go about, to get properly dressed, and walk a bit, and it was dreadfully exhausting, deadly uninteresting. But to lie on a rug in the sunshine and poke in the ground with weeder or trowel or fingers, wasn't in the least tiring, it was wonderfully exciting. And the moment I cared to I could rest just where I was—pull the pillow under my head and watch the birds. I suppose it's the way a baby begins—creeps, and does things, and then drops his toy as soon as he's tired. And then when I tried to walk, I found I'd been growing some muscle in my back, and that it felt no longer like a wet string. There was real muscle in it. You won't believe me, but I helped Clarky put those stones in place and make the wall before I'd walked as far as the barn. Oh, yes, it was the gardening. That and Stephen McLeod."

"Who's Stephen McLeod?"

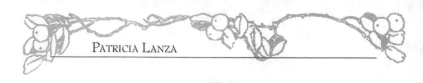

"Stephen McLeod? He is a curious fellow who comes up here every Sunday. He has stock in the pasture above—you may see him when you go up the hill—he haunts it. He looks a little like your patron saint. 'Appleseed Johnny.'"

"What did he have to do with your getting well?"

"Lots. I can't tell exactly; but he did. He makes you feel as if you were only a little part of a very great life, as if in all the out-of-doors was an immense and wonderful force that enfolded you. And it rests you, just like when you were little and things went wrong, and your mother took you in her arms. The fret and the trouble go out, and the quietness and the strength come in. I don't know how it happens, but it does happen, and the touch of the earth has something to do with it. You feel as if the things that had concerned you were curiously unimportant beside the sky and the birds and the growing things, and you come in touch with the wonderful patience of the old earth."

"However it was brought about," said he, "I'm delighted at the result." Then silence.

Suddenly I had that curious warning sensation that every woman knows, somewhere in the back of one's head or hair (our inheritance, I suppose, from the prehistoric days when a man's attentions consisted of dragging one by the hair or whacking one over the head with a club), while clear before my eyes as if it were present, instead of the apple tree and the wide stretch of green, was the old garden of the Protheroes just as it looked on a day three years ago. June, it was, and early in the morning, too. And Richard had made me come over to see his roses, and he stood by the sun dial at the end of the garden and touched the little Wichuraianas that had climbed to it's face. His hand trembled a little as he touched them while he asked me what I wished he had not. The thin brown hand that laid beside me now on the seamed, weather-beaten threshold trembled a little. I came back to the present with a start. Richard was speaking.

"But I didn't come altogether for the orchards," he was saying; "that was in the nature of a—pretext. Do you remember what I asked you three years ago?" he ended abruptly.

"Yes," I said slowly, "I remember, but I feel like a wholly different person, Richard, like a snake that has sloughed his skin—-"

"Then, you may feel differently," he said, "about that. People change, ideas—modify. I have cared for you for a long time," he said simply.

"But I'm not the sort you want, Richard," I protested uncomfortably. "It should be someone, with some life and force, and energy. I haven't courage to take up so—demanding a life. I couldn't! I couldn't face parishioners; any time they worried my roots, I should just succumb, like the plants with the cutworms! It's humiliating, but it's true. I couldn't."

"Those are excuses," said Richard quietly. "not reasons. What's the reason? Don't you care at all?" He laid one thin brown hand on mine, and at that I turned and faced the large lenses which were rather terrifying just then.

"Not that way," I answered. "Don't you see, it's just because we've been neighbors and friends for so long that you think of —of this sort of thing. Propinquity makes no end of trouble. You can care for some one else very differently, so that it would be an utterly different thing. I know it."

"How do you know it?" said Richard quickly, and a bit suspiciously.

Whereat I was idiotic enough to colour, as people often do for nothing at all. But Richard looked at me still more suspiciously. He started to say something, but what it was I don't know, for just at that moment Clarky came around the corner by the lilac bush with the milk-can in her hand. She was a bit flushed from her walk, and her thick boots were soaking.

"How early we all are!" said she briskly. "Have you been catching worms, Mr. Protheroe?"

"I am bound for the old orchard, Miss Clarke," he said. "I have no doubt there are worms in abundance there. If you are planning a fishing excursion, I will bring you some, though I had intended leaving them for the woodpeckers."

"Why didn't you keep him for a proper breakfast?" said Clarky disappointedly, as Richard took his way up

the hill. "I know Mrs. Tarbox has given him nothing but pie for his lunch—pie and perhaps layer-cake. That's not suitable nourishment for an all-day tramp. I certainly hope his experiment works. It's as rare to see a clergyman trying his percepts as it is to see a physician willing to take his own medicine and submit to his preferred operation. Administering is so much more pleasant."

Chapter
Twenty-One

Richard was by no means as disconsolate as it seemed to me he ought to have been. Rather, he appeared relieved; his spirits, instead of being heavier, grew perceptibly lighter. Until I began to wonder if Aunt Cassandra had put into his head any extraordinary ideas about my being in a languishing condition because of blighted affection. You can count on your friends, but you never can tell what relatives are likely to do; they often feel empowered to act for you and to think for you, and yet they know you less than any one of your acquaintance. Wherein lies the nucleus of many a family quarrel.

But to return to Richard Protheroe. He prolonged, instead of curtailing, his visit. He stayed two weeks more with Mrs. Tarbox, nor did he shun our hill. Instead, he came up it every day. He sat on Clarky's bench below the lilac bush and had tea with us. He stayed for dinner or supper whenever he was asked. He said our whole scheme of life was "distinctly Ardenic"; that our housekeeping reminded him of Rosalind's and Celia's. "But what a pity they had no fireless cooker." The odd fellow who haunted the woods, he conceived to be Orlando; he said he firmly expected to find panegyrics hunk upon the trees and had already begun to look for them. And he called Mrs. Tarbox Audrey, behind her back, of course; he said she had that Shakespearian character's literalness and passion for the exact, the concrete. Also that Audrey was the true type of the native countrywoman, while the others of "As You Like It" were dilettante.

He grew quite interested in my garden, although, like Clarky, he didn't take it as seriously as I could have wished. He admired my mound of blossoming squash vines encircled by cornflowers, and said it would have delighted William Morris with it's combination of the Useful and Beautiful.

Mrs. Tarbox didn't altogether approve of the Reverend Richard. She thought he came up our hill too much. She eyed him severely when he talked of "prospecting" and she told me afterward that "ef he'd give Mis' Pritchard a good account of his prospects 'twould be more to the p'int." Also, she held that a young clergyman should't gallivant.

It did not seem to me that working in my garden could be described as gallivanting, and Richard really did put in some work. He cut saplings from the beechwoods and helped Clarky set up poles for the beans, which were fairly clamoring for assistance and stretching out frantically, with long, swaying shoots, to find something to help them skyward. After the poles were set, he cut other saplings, made cross poles of them, lashing them in place with string, and constructed a rude pergola, "to carry out your William Morris effect," said he. One rainy day he and Clarky had a beautiful time in the woodshed at the workbench making frames for starting perennials.

Clarky is really a surgical nurse, which is why she so loves a saw and hammer, I suppose. She and the Reverend Richard did the work, and they did it with joy and energy.

I sat on the doorstep and watched, and offered suggestions. There's nothing more delightful than to witness other people working for your garden when you have the pleasing assurance that the work is being properly done. So I sat and watched them hammering and sawing, and looked out of the wide door toward the distant hemlocks and watched the gusts of mist and rain hurrying by the trees and up the hill, like a ghostly army in silent flight.

The frames were interesting. Richard had brought down from the barn a motley array of old boards that he and Clarky had found in the attic—-old window sashes from which every pane of glass had long been absent. They made the frames to fit the window sashes—that is, the size of a window. The height of the frame at the back was a foot and a half, and at the front a foot, so that the sash had the proper professional slope. They tacked cheesecloth over the sashes.

"The florists use lath," said Richard, "but this will serve. All you need is a little shade. Young perennials, in a state of nature, come up slightly under the shadow of their parent's leaves, and we have to simulate the natural environment."

He told me how, in the autumn, I could set glass in the sashes and have a sure-enough cold-frame. He said he thought the farmers in our part of the world were mildly insane not to use their storm windows as a sash for coldframes from March until Christmas time and sell forced vegetables to summer residents.

"Not insanity," said Clarky, "merely arrested development, Mr. Protheroe."

Next day the frames were properly set east of the woodshed, where they had a little shelter from the north and west. The soil was made light and smooth, and then I did the planting: sweet William, Canterbury bells and larkspur and hollyhocks, monkshood, China pinks. The larkspur were a dark blue "hybridum" and a pale blue

"coelestinum"; the hollyhocks were all single varieties. Richard said they were less liable to disease and also more decorative. Pansies I had, too, and platycodon and little English daisies.

It was Richard who insisted on the hardy plants. He said annuals were very well, but they were to a garden as summer boarders to a town—useful, but by no means taking the place of year-round residents. He said he couldn't for the life of him see why green-gardeners always began operations with roses and annuals, which were like starting chicken raising with incubator chickens, when one might have the maternal services of a worthy hen and be spared much anxiety and responsibility. He said that bulbs and perennials and shrubs were infinitely easier to manage, but never did a green gardener try them! He told me that my little perennials that I was starting in July would be ready to go to their permanent homes in late September; that they would then be on hand in the spring with but little further care from me. I could have sown lots more, but I didn't know what I would do with them.

"You'll have abundance to give away, as it is," said the Reverend Richard. "That's half the fun of gardening. Wait till you see the garden I have! I'm going to make an Elisabethan `Flowery Orchard' of that old orchard beyond the church, and the children will come from miles around to beg for the flowers."

"You haven't had your `call' yet," said I.

"I shall have it, my dear Caroline," said he. "If the people will not give me the usual five hundred, I shall offer to come for four hundred and nighty-eight. I shall have tea-parties in my garden, and the nice old ladies who come will get the habit and make a pretty bit of garden themselves for the same purpose. They will come to me for slips and cuttings and young plants."

"But the time," I said, "how can you possible do it?"

"Judicious management and autumn planting," said he. "Gardening consists not so much in a wild frenzy of industry in the spring as in doing odd bits of work at the proper time—"here a little and there a little." In doing things, not so much when others sleep, as when they do not think about it. The difficulty in which the Foolish

Virgins found themselves was not that the oil for the lamps was impossible to obtain; it would have been a most simple matter had they done the work at the proper time. But most people garden after the manner of the Foolish Virgins and rush frantically about the work when the season has already begun. Such, I believe, was your method."

"Besides," he continued, "I may bring two or three Juvenile Delinquents to assist."

"But how could you possibly look after two or three young imps besides your garden?"

"That will be the interesting part, my dear Caroline. If I can show a creditable and a profitable garden and yet have a little leisure, and if I can show young sinners fairer and fatter and of better behavior than the more properly pedigreed children of the neighborhood, then I shall be in a position to express an opinion on the community problems. And if I cannot do the trick, why exhort?"

Chapter Twenty-Two

We missed Richard, after he went back to civilization, more than I had supposed we should. Especially did Clark miss him. He was terribly energetic like herself. Besides the coldframes and the beanpole pergola, they made a bridge of fallen logs across the little brook, cut the dead wood from some of the trees in the old orchard, and made one of the darling old things spruce with a Spartan severity—as sanitary as a hospital.

I am not sure it really liked the change. I have always had a notion that, however bad it is for the bodies, these old trees must find their spirits enlivened by the multitudinous life around and about and over them; that the pines must take an interest in the squirrels that make their houses under the roots, in the high-hole woodpeckers that carve abodes for themselves far aloft; and that the apple trees must rather like the visits of the woodpeckers who tap them over as assiduously as an osteopath looking for a defect— and if there were not borers or other insects to reward them—but this is rank heresy, I know! I suppose it comes from watching the woodpeckers until one gets their viewpoint. Certainly, when insects worried my garden, their aspect changed.

But my garden wasn't suffering. For almost the first time I could survey it without seeing forty things that I ought to do and hadn't done. I began to feel as the barn swallows must have felt when their brood had got past the gaping mouth stage and the clamor for incessant attention, and the parents could watch with more or less calmness and criticize the flying process. Hitherto, I had been able to do nothing but try, rather frantically, to keep the plants from being killed by something or crowded into ill health. Now I could look about with a bit of detachment and consider the garden as an artistic creation, something in the way I fondly regarded it when I lay on my back and planned, with the catalogues to help, and no distressing realities to worry. I could consider now, with some degree of placidity, whether hollyhocks would look better here, or there; for the young plants were growing contentedly in the frames, and might stay there all winter without injury—a very different matter from deciding where to put them when the May sun is beating down perilously hot, and the young things are lying in a packing-box, roots out of the ground, as clamorous for their native element as a fish out of water.

Clarky says a first garden is like a first baby. The parents get terribly excited over the least indisposition and think it's in imminent peril at the slightest woe, but when it's the second, or third, or forth infant, they take a wail of distress more calmly. They know the variety of the wail, and precisely what to do!

So now, when I sat on the bench below the lilac bush, I began to consider the garden critically and to think far nobler and pleasanter to contemplate than rose bugs or swarming aphides.

I sat and gazed down the bean walk now garlanded in real pergola fashion and thought it needed a better finish than the poles against the distant mountains; something tall and straight and green, like Italian cypresses, one at each side just inside the line of posts.

I confided this idea to Clarky.

"Shucks!" she said (Clarky has picked up some expressions from Mrs. Tarbox), "this isn't Italy. Isn't it enough to have your garden grow and the plants healthy and —normal?"

Then I tried Stephen. He was more hopeful.

"Something tall and straight and green," he said musingly. "There are young junipers in the pasture that would be that. We could get them where they would be spared easy. And for the corners of the beds, young pines would be all right for a few years. It's too cold here for box. Want to come?"

"Where?"

"Up the hill to find them."

"Of course."

Next morning he brought the horses.

Chapter Twenty-Three

It so happened, that, although I had been four months at the little house, never yet had I gone up the hill. I suppose the reason was that my heart was still a bit queer; nothing serious, only it like to sit down, which made hill climbing a nuisance. So my walks had chiefly been along the level, grassed road and across the brook to the wonderful pasture; and Stephen McLeod, for all his promise, had never yet taken me up his hill.

He came that morning with the same wagon he had that first May day. Only he had blankets in it and a seat back rigged of rope laced across the rough stakes to make me comfortable: and he had burlap for the comfort of the plants, and a spade to dig them with. Slowly we went up the long, open slope, crashing through the tall goldenrod; then we passed through the red gate and entered the pine road. Here Stephen got out and walked.

Up and up went the road, straight up through the pines—tall, straight, branchless trunks, the dark tops touching and forming a canopy high overhead, like the pines in a Southern forest; and high overhead the tops swayed and murmured to each other although the slender seedling dandelion the wagon grazed never stirred.

Underfoot the red-brown pine needles, undisturbed these fifty years, lay thick and soft like a deep-piled carpet; through it little hard ferns thrust their sharp fronds; here and there a late Canada violet bloomed alone, or a solitary dandelion grown oddly tall and slender; a bit of Herb Robert fringed the edge by the heavy rail fence with a wood aster swaying above it as lightly as a columbine. Right under the horse's feet grew the stiff little heal-all, more slender than in the open and almost a gentian blue.

The horses stopped to rest, for the road was very steep.

"Your New Englanders would think it morally wrong, I suppose," I said, "to leave the old property line where the road has always been and take the hill at a zigzag to get a better grade for the horses. It might be an evasion of hardship! Yet one would get to the top all the same and about as quickly."

"You don't understand the New Englanders," said Stephen. "They are rather like their hills—bleak and uncompromising and forbidding most of the time. But there are wonderful moments—there's a sudden beauty and poetry, and exquisite moment—and then it goes. But you remember it! The people are like that. There is a rareness and a fineness. Once in a long while you see it; but having seen it you never forget it and always you know it is there.

"Look back," he said.

I turned. One could have fancied one's self looking

through a forest of masts to the blue sea, for through the straight, close assembled trunks showed the blue of the distant mountains and nothing in between.

"It's curious," he said, "that people are content to shut themselves in houses and tie up their lives with things and never go to the woods except to murder them or the wild life in them, or else with a crowd on a picnic." He laughed whimsically. "The trees know better than to say anything to them; they talk to you if you go to them alone."

"What is it you do up here, Stephen McLeod?" I said. "It's never stock raising you do on these hills. Is it poetry? Or mustn't I ask?"

He looked at me—the quick, startled look—then scrutinized me a moment, intently, penetratingly; hesitated a bit, then:

"I'll show you," he said. "I've half intended to show you for a long time. We're near there now."

He turned from the pine road into an open trackless pasture. I saw no vestige of a road, but presently we entered woods again and were on a road, straight and

level, but so overgrown that the crowding hemlocks brushed the wagon wheels and bent over and touched our faces; and far ahead the opening showed the blue tip of the mountain. Stephen stopped the horses, helped me down, pushed aside the branches, and I saw a crazy little shack, the key of which he carried in his canvas pocket.

It was a small, bare room that I entered. There was a tiny chunk stove; at one side a rough bench under a narrow window high up on one side; in one corner was an old easel; standing crowded against the wall was canvas after canvas. He picked one up, looked at it a second, flushed a bit, then he set it on the easel and moved it so that the light was right; then he took it away and put on another and another. He had painted the mountain again and again, each time with a varying aspect. Now as he told me of it first with the slender columbine against the sea of mist that almost hid it, then in the deep blue of October and the wonderful mauves and purples of the October twilight, the work had a vigor and freshness and subtlety, too.

"If you take a beautiful thing and isolate it, sometimes you can make people see it," he said, "see that it is beautiful, just as one takes a stone and puts it in a setting. To me that is the whole point of art—if one sees that the thing is beautiful one must make it evident to people who would not see otherwise."

"Look at my view," he said, breaking off. He made me stand on the bench and look out of his wide window. Below was sheer cliff—his fortress was a Gibraltar from that side. Far, very far below I could see my little house with the wide green slope—much greener than the surrounding pasture—and the line of trees at it's back, the elm beside it—all looking like a German toy, the trees unreal like toy trees.

"Do you see your place?" asked Stephen. I nodded.

"What is it you are going to do to it," he said, jealously. "It's a dear little place; this is the only spot from which you can see it. Your not going to make an Italian garden, surely!"

"I'm not planning anything very dreadful," I said. "I only want to bring down some columbines. I'd rather

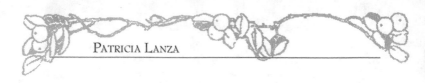

have the wild ones than the others. And then I don't like the look of the bean poles against the divine blue that the mountain is now; I want two junipers for just inside. I'm going to mark the corners of the flower-beds with chubby little pines, so that I won't lose them—I mean lose track of just where they are during the winter. There's nothing very iconoclastic in that, is there?"

Stephen laughed. "No," he said, "I like a garden. But where the country's so beautiful we have less need; don't tie yourself up with your garden. The woods are never so lovely as they are in May. I must show them to you next year, so don't make a garden that isn't able to take care of itself in the early spring. That's the kind I have.

"What do you mean?"

"Oh, bulbs. They can shift for themselves beautifully, and like to. I put mine a foot deep so that annuals on top won't trouble them. They don't mind the extra climb. Just have things that are strong and sturdy, and if you want roses, have the wild kinds. Save the early spring for the scarlet maples and make all your garden now!"

Stephen locked the little place and we walked a

bit down the road, for he said there were columbines just below.

"But can you spare them?" I asked.

He laughed. "There are oceans of them here," he said, "or even you shouldn't have them."

He dug them carefully and showed me how to wrap the roots; then we went down the hill after the junipers. Fat little pines we found, too, and violet plants for Clarky's garden. Stephen told me how I could make a houseplant of a hemlock by keeping it very wet for a few days and in the shade.

The road came out by another old orchard, and Stephen showed me the line of the old foundations and the terrace—all there was left of the house; for otherwise there was no sign, except for the tansy growing riotously in a square patch. It had usurped all the old herb bed.

"Some one here has liked the junipers for decoration," said he, and he showed me four huge clumps of the spreading juniper set at regular intervals below the terrace line.

"Where have the people gone, and who were they?" I said.

"Don't know," he answered. "Our country is full of places like this. Some-times there's a wreck of a house left—your place would have been that in another dozen years—oftener the house is gone completely. It's only the hills and the little bluets that are really permanent," he said.

Chapter Twenty-Four

I had a beautiful time over my garden making. Gardening in late September is a very different thing from the planting done late in May, in frantic haste. Then Mother Nature herself seems in a very frenzy of industry, like a New England housewife bent on spring cleaning. Even the days are longer then, as if the sun had been especially requested to give a little more time for work.

Now everything went in leisurely fashion. The days were quiet and golden; as quiet as at the creation when the "evening and the morning" made the day, each suddenly overtaken by darkness that dropped like a quick

curtain. The thrushes were silent; the fox-sparrow and the humming birds flitted about quietly with nothing of the desperate haste that had been theirs earlier; the bluebirds in the apple tree were thinking of their winter flight and resting for their great adventure. What tiny things to have such high-hearted courage! What brave explorers and what passionate homemakers! How they must despise us as incompetents who are so craven about getting away from our accustomed haunts and away from the base of supplies!

My woodpecker has no intention of leaving; he taps, taps, as assiduously as ever—to have the tree ready for the next tenants, I suppose. Sometimes he taps at my window in the mornings; he just happens by and does it from force of habit!

I worked peacefully and slowly in my garden, planting carefully, and watering properly, and I followed my handsome plan. I had a broad, central path, long beds each side, the plants in rows for convenient weeding. Farthest back I set hollyhocks—the young plants from my frames—for they could look over the heads of the others without difficulty. In front of them came Canterbury bells, and I made an edge of little English daisies. And where ever there was space (and wherever there wasn't) I sowed Shirley poppies, to my mind the most exquisite of all the flowers that ever grew. Why is it that even the poets have blackened its character? "The poppy's red effrontery." I believe that was Robert Browning; and someone else speaks of its color as "flaunting." Flaunting! When no flower has more of the spirit and less of the earth. How can they misunderstand it's marvelous delicacy and lightness of poise; so sure, and so wonderfully slender of stem that it seems like color incarnate rather than a product of growth of leaf and stalk and stem! Then its bursting from the sheath like an imprisoned sprite and letting its crumpled petals smooth in the sun as a newborn butterfly dries its wings. No flower is so instinct with life. And all this life and color and beauty content to spring from the poorest soil and the hardest conditions! It's a poet and artist by nature. And the roses, belauded and petted for centuries as types of maiden innocence and loveliness, must have

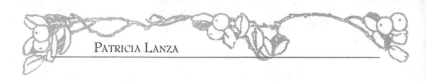
heavy feeding and constant attention or they will do nothing at all! It's an odd world and ungrateful one!

So I scratched the soil where the grass grew thin and planted poppies there that might grow up in the grass. I set the tall, straight junipers where they "looked right," at the end of the path with the mountain behind them, and the fat little pines marked the corners of my beds quite as well as if they had been box plants. I had grown, by this time, quite expert at planting; I brought Virginia creeper from the woods and set it against the house, and I planted the columbines and violets we had brought down from the hill in among the maidenhair ferns in the bed with the retaining wall that Clarky had made.

I worked slowly and happily, and in no frantic fashion. I suppose the quiet and patience of the hills sinks into one and gets under the skin. Then, when I stopped work, there was the mountain to look at that was quietness itself and very rich in its royal purple. Indeed, all gold and purple the landscape seemed. Goldenrod held the sunshine in the pasture; marigolds were blooming happily in the garden; and up the hill, out from among the dark pines, flashed here and there the early crimson of a scarlet maple—as vivid as a pennant flung out to catch the eye.

Then I watched the cattle, which, if there is anything in "suggestion," are enough to make the most febrile person take life quietly. To me there came to be something quiet admirable in the calmness with which these bovine neighbors of ours took life. Those cows could stand and gaze at me for twenty minutes straight—until I felt oddly embarrassed; gaze with a godlike impassivity and chew without having to stop and bite as the horses did. Nothing interrupted the calm stare and the slow, steady motion of the jaws.

Richard Protheroe said he believed the general rural prevalence of the tobacco chewing habit was chiefly due to "suggestion" from the cows. But Richard is rather frivolous for a clergyman.

Clarky says it would be charming to see the cows coming down the hill at evening into our barn.

"It's far better that they come down into some one else's barn, Clarky," I said. "Cows would mean milking, and milking, a hired man, and with a hired man would go our solitude. A cow on the landscape suggests contemplation; in the barn, it suggests chores. It's far better to have the effect of the cattle on the landscape and get our milk from the Thistledown Farm."

But Clarky would insist that they were an essential part of rural life. "No well-equipped farm could exist without them; and did I not think the Holstein-Friesian a better all-around cow than the Jersey, which was too liable to tuberculosis?" Clarky had gotten amazingly interested in farming and live stock. She seemed to have lost interest in my garden now that the manual training stage had passed and the carpenter work was lacking. But all along she had rather regarded it as safe amusement and a hygienic one rather than the serious work it was. She woke up a little when Richard Protheroe sent a box of bulbs, and showed me how to plant them properly and set each one on a cushion of sand.

"It prevents a kind of Rheumatism," said she.

We planted Darwin Tulips and, down in the grass under the apple trees and beside the doorstep and at the foot of the big lilac, crocuses and snowdrops. These might blossom, I knew, before I could come back, but they would keep the little house company until the lilac bush broke into bloom.

We had delightful evenings, clear and cool, with the crackling fire indoors for company and the chirping of the crickets outside. Sometimes we would be off on the hills and not come back until long after dusk had fallen and made the familiar path wonderful with a strange, unreal beauty.

But Clarky was too full of rural problems to take these loafing rambles restfully enough. She wanted to reform the old orchards that we passed and, in her mind, stopped and pruned them so that they should bear fruit and be useful instead of abandoning themselves to the busy, restless swarm of insect life and bird life that to me they seemed contentedly mothering. Clarky talked rural sanitation and instruction in cooking and nursing and handicraft—useful indeed, I admit, but too stimulating—and I had grown in love with loafing. Besides, had I not a right? Was I not a sure-enough

invalid perfectly entitled to months of convalescence? I had had the discomforts of illness, now I proposed to have the joys, whereof and almost infantine freedom from a sense of responsibility is the chief.

So I let Clarky write her plans of parish reform to Richard Protheroe and I went up the hill with Stephen to fetch pineneedles for my garden's winter bedding, and we brought down cones for the fireplace, all of which was eminently useful, to my mind, as arranging the lives and digestions for a community who really seemed quite content without such aid.

Stephen, apparently, had another attack of pressing business up the hill, like the one which sent him logging in the spring just when the hill was loveliest. We would go up the hill with the horses, then leave them, and walk across through the woods. I had grown stronger by now, and could walk mile after mile through the golden woods, if I had the "lift" up the hill. Stephen was painting a bit of the forest he loved with a color and feeling which it seemed should make the beauty of it visible to any but the blind.

It was now October, and the gold and purple had left the open and withdrawn to the hills; the woods were all golden, clear and still, the air fine and sharp and went to one's head like wine; the leaves were crisp underfoot and the feathery young hemlocks seemed awake and alive as never before.

In my forest, the level beechwoods where the thrushes lived, was a carpet of coppery beech leaves, and high overhead a few dark pines mingled their tops with the slow, dull, magnificent crimson of the great oak trees.

In October Madame Nature seems to take a wicked, mischievous delight in trying to stir the senses of the New Englander with a sudden, almost shameless flaunting of her gorgeous beauty—up and down his hills, round and about, under his feet and over his head, as if she were trying to wake a bit of passion for herself in his chill and unresponsive breast. But for the most part, he remains a very St. Anthony.

Stephen McLeod and I made excursions through the woods, walking mile after mile in a silence that was broken only by the crackling of twigs underfoot—

under my foot usually, for Stephen walked with the silence and sureness of an Indian. Again and again we would come on one of those wonderful garden-spots, sheltered places, curiously warm, where odd little summer lingers as if by enchantment—now a rock side with moss as green and dripping as if it were May and the courageous little Herb Robert snatching a scant foothold and blossoming as if there had been no such thing as frost to turn the goldenrod to ashes and snap the maple leaves. Sometimes we came so close to a partridge that I could see its markings as plainly as if it had been a barnyard fowl, and the quick, sensitive head, which never a barnyard fowl possesses, and makes one wonder if domestication had really improved—except in the matter of flesh.

Then we would have a Robinson Crusoe luncheon of beechnuts and some curious flat pine kernels and coffee made over an incredibly small fire that was carefully extinguished before we "broke camp".

Then down the hill we would come, the wagon piled with bags of needles and cones for the fire, facing a sunset that flamed crimson through the dark pine trunks.

Often Stephen would stay for supper, sit and smoke by the fire with the kitten curled on his knee, and Clarky, being industrious, would sew. She was making some nurse's big aprons. I suppose, if I had been a creditable specimen of womankind I would have sewed also, but I had watched the cows too long. Besides, no one can loaf like an active person who once gets the habit, and I was recovering from the vice of over-industry.

Sometimes Stephen would pull a book out of his pocket and read. Keats or Shelley he would be likely to have in the big pocket of that canvas coat, or some of "Paradise Lost." He liked the grandeur of the slow-moving lines very much as he liked his mountain. But he never read any of these to Clarky. I think the rural sanitation alarmed him for his favorites, although Shelly, surely, would have been interested in the subject. Instead, he read John Woolman, that curiously practical idealist, or else the charming "Letters of an American Farmer," an out-of-print, before-the-Revolution, book.

It was easy to understand why he liked it, for Hector St. John de Crevecoeur must have been a farmer after Stephen's own heart, with his keen sense of the color and beauty, and his care, on winter mornings, that their feet might not become chilled while breakfasting.

The wild pigeon, which, in Crevecoeur's time were evidently as abundant as English sparrows in town, have disappeared completely. What a pity we must always bring a trail of slaughter and destruction! Stephen holds with John Woolman that we must take care "not to diminish the sweetness of life to any living creature."

Chapter
Twenty-Five

So went October and November, the days unhurried and wonderful, but the weeks rushed by (according to the calendar) with a startling rapidity. The woods were no longer golden, but brown; the birds were gone, the summer resident birds; the deer mice were busy making homes for themselves; the squirrels were terribly industrious, busy and chattering over their nut getting. They had evidently played all summer, and this was the serious business of the year.

I was ready for the winter, too. My garden was snugly covered. Hollyhocks and all the others were carefully

blanketed with the pine needles, with evergreen boughs laid on top as a quilt to keep them in place.

There was scant excuse for staying longer in the little house—it was undeniably cold in the mornings—but still we lingered. Clarky was getting restless. She had loafed all the "loaf" that was in her and she wanted to get to work on a real case. Besides, Richard Protheroe kept writing to her volumes on rural sanitation in its relation to the ministry, and up-to-date orcharding; and he wanted, so she said, to advise with her how best he could make the old parsonage beside his flowery orchard into a model of sanitary excellence and modern improvement. "Tell him to live in the orchard!" Stephen said, "It's much pleasanter." I thought Clarky rather disproportionately interested in that parsonage.

At last she began to pack. I went and sat on the doorstep disconsolately. I had on the same lumberman's leggings and moccasins that Clarky had got for me at first, for the cold was unmistakable and already we had had little flurries of snow. I heard Clarky pulling and hauling trunks about and really enjoying the activity.

I sat there in the November sunshine, warm, if it was a bit reluctant, and looked about. The hills stretched brown and rather disconsolate, also; the grass was dead, never a woodchuck sat at his house door for every one of them had been a month or more in his warm burrow, spending the winter season in the underworld like a furry Proserpina. The big gray squirrel was scolding and chattering in the woodshed. He wanted us to go; I know he intended to establish himself in the attic the second we were out of the house. Our red-headed woodpecker was tapping busily; he had no intention of going away and didn't care in the least whether we stayed or went. Probably he'd be tapping with the same unconcern when we came back.

Suddenly Stephen appeared.

"You are really going?" he asked.

I nodded. "Clarky's packing, don't you hear her?" I said, for within the house a truck lid fell with a bang.

Stephen's face clouded, then it cleared suddenly. "But you aren't packing," he said. "There's a wonderful little place over in the pasture yonder," he pointed south

over the wide, grassed stretch, "that has forgotten the time of year. Won't you come? I want to show it to you."

The sky cleared for me, also, as we went over the brown grassed road, past the barns, past the red gate and into the pasture that was brown and bare as the leafless maple trees, the ashen tops of dead goldenrod and the stiff, brown spearheads of the spires. Instead of going up the hill, he led the way down to a little circular group of young pines standing close together in a tiny amphitheatre. Once within the enclosure and November had vanished. The ground was level; the red-brown of the pine needles was threaded with ground pine and soft with moss, and over it all and through it all was the little Herb Robert, it's fragile, delicate loveliness untroubled by the calendar, the tiny rose-colored blossoms as gaily erect as if there were no such thing as frost.

I sat down on the moss and took some of the dear little flowers between my fingers, but I didn't break them. They were such courageous little things, they must live as long as they could. Stephen stood looking at the river in silence. Then he came and sat beside me. The clouds were over the mountain and turned it's purple into a dull violet. The winding river far below us looked dark and sullen, almost black. Perhaps it also would have preferred not to go down to the city.

"Must you go?" he asked.

"I'm afraid so," I answered.

"The woods are wonderful here in the winter," he said. "The stillness of them and the whiteness of them! And you go through early in the morning after a snowfall before even the squirrels have dug out their houses. And the color! Such reds in the pine trunks and such vividness in the hemlocks! They seem aloof in the summer and half awake, but they are wonderfully alive then. They talk to you."

"I wish I could see it," I said.

"I suppose it calls you, the other life," Stephen said slowly.

"It doesn't call me. But there are things I must do, now I'm well. And there are people—"

"Once, last year, when I was over at your place," he said irrelevantly, "a deer had been killed near your apple tree; there was blood on the snow. And in March I found eighteen or twenty little fox-sparrows dead from cold and hunger in our woods, they had come too early. Neither of those things would have happened had you been here! Are there people who so greatly need you?" he asked eagerly.

I thought of Aunt Cassandra, who held a little oversight of me necessary as an unwelcome chore, and of my brother Rod vastly occupied with his engagement. "There's no one in such urgent need," I said, "but I ought to go."

"You've been happy in this life?" He said.

"Very. I never was really happy before."

He hesitated a moment. Then he turned to me with a sudden directness, and the shyness dropped, as it always did when he spoke what he felt. "I have waited for you all my life," he said; "Why didn't you come before," and now that you've come, why do you speak of going?"

"I did not know—-"I said. And then I looked at him, and before the light in his face my eyes fell, but I felt something strange and wonderful wake in me—as wonderful as it must be to the maples when the frost lets go and the sap rushes through every vein to waken it. And then—

But I shall not write what was said then. That belongs to Stephen, and to me, and to the darling little flowers that looked up at us both—wondering aloof. They had heard that story before; it was old to them and the hill. Life and love and birth and death, the old mystery and the old sweetness, and the very houses that had sheltered were gone.

"This one winter I must go back," I said, in answer to Stephen's question, as we turned our faces homeward in the dusk.

"But in the spring, very early in the spring—?, he urged.

"In the spring." I said.

"Before the scarlet maples and the bloodroot," I assented. "We can be up at the little house together."

"I know now why I so loved your little place," said Stephen, abruptly.

It is now the middle of December; we have been home three weeks from the little house. I've been sitting at my window in the old room where I used to sit when I was ill, looking over the journal I tried to keep of the summer's adventure. Down in the yard next door Uncle Hermann is covering his rosebushes with straw. He has on the same short, thick jacket that makes him look rounder than ever, and the pockets are still bulging with string and shears as when in February he began pruning the vines and set me off a-gardening.

Ah, Uncle Hermann! Where should I be now if you hadn't cared about your roses and pruned them so assiduously? Still as limp and useless as a seedling with a cutworm at its root? I wonder! But your roses are going to wake up in the spring and I shall be very wide-awake in the spring. Stephen and I are going to see it, together, from the first flush of the scarlet maples until the leaves are out on the lilac bush.

But it seems a bit long to wait for the scarlet maples!

The End

Epilogue

After all the reading it takes to bring a book to publication, plus all the reading I did for the pure pleasure this book brings, I still love this little book and once it is bound will most likely read it many more times. So it feels good to know you will be able to read it also.

Except for the picture on the cover, Herb Robert growing in one of my gardens, I have kept to the original printing, letting the words draw pictures for you. In every reading I found something I could relate to; being ill, getting well in my garden, loving poppies and feeling them much aligned and finding a good man to share my life with.

I have been where Caroline was; overworked, ill, feeling my life was hanging by a thread and feeling a burden to family. I had my own window to look out and from that window found a passion that helped me get my life back. My gardens brought the people that helped change my life to me and my passion drove me from the loneliness of my room out into the world where I came back to life and eventually..love.

During the growing season I live for the time I spend in the garden and when the season is over I retreat to my room with the most wonderful view. From there I write all about the people and plants that come and go in my life that keeps it interesting.

It was almost twenty years since I drove down the mountain to the library book sale and found "My Garden Doctor". A lot has happened in twenty years but, in many ways, I am still the same, just older. If longevity is a test then this little book is still a winner just as my love of it has endured, even grown.

Enjoy!

Other books by Patricia Lanza:

Recipes from New England's Best Inns and
Bed & Breakfasts,
> Readers Digest

How to Create Wonderful Gardens,
with No Digging, No Tilling, No Kidding!,
> Smidt Press

Lasagna Gardening, No Digging, No Tilling, No
Weeding, No Kidding! Rodale Press
Lasagna Gardening for Small Spaces,
> Rodale Press

Lasagna Gardening with Herbs,
> Rodale Press

My Grandmother's Aprons
(essay in My Mother's Garden)
> Penguin Press

LaVergne, TN USA
03 April 2011
222647LV00001B/2/P